182 Greek Words

The Language of the New Testament Bible

182 Greek Words

The Language of the New Testament Bible

Vinu V Das

TP
Tabor Press

ISBN 978-0-9940194-8-6

Table of Contents

Introduction

Welcome to *182 Greek Words: The Language of the New Testament Bible*, a journey into the heart of Scripture through its original language. This book is designed to open new dimensions of understanding as you explore the foundational Greek words that shape the message of the New Testament.

Learning the language in which the New Testament was written can transform your Bible study experience. Each word has been chosen for its theological significance and its ability to reveal the depth of God's message. Whether you are a seasoned scholar or a curious seeker, this resource offers insights that invite a closer, more personal relationship with the text. The original Greek not only enhances comprehension but also invites you to experience the vibrancy and nuance of the Gospel as it was first proclaimed.

As you read through this book, you will find that every word serves as a key to unlocking profound theological truths and spiritual insights. You will gain clarity on terms that, in translation, sometimes lose the richness of the original language. This study is not merely academic—it is an invitation to let the Word of God reshape your heart and mind, to see familiar passages in a new light, and to appreciate the timeless beauty of Scripture.

The journey through these 182 words is both a challenge and a gift. It challenges you to engage deeply with the language, to uncover the layers of meaning beneath each term, and to apply these insights to your everyday life. At the same time, it is a gift that equips you with tools for a richer, more informed devotion. As you reflect on each word, may you find your understanding of God's truth deepened and your passion for His Word renewed.

May this book serve as a stepping stone into a vibrant, dynamic relationship with God's Word, enriching your study, deepening your faith, and transforming your walk with Christ. Welcome to a journey of discovery that will illuminate the path of truth and grace as you engage with the language that has shaped the hearts of believers for millennia.

Week 1 Theme: Christian Virtues

Christian Virtues: A Life Reflecting Christ

Christian virtues are the foundation of a life that reflects the character of Christ. They are not just moral principles but expressions of a heart transformed by God's grace. Love, faith, humility, patience, kindness, and self-control are among the many virtues that shape a believer's daily walk with God. These qualities are not achieved through human effort alone but are cultivated by the work of the Holy Spirit in our lives (Galatians 5:22-23).

Living out Christian virtues means embodying Christ's love in our relationships, showing compassion to those in need, and walking in integrity in all we do. It requires patience in trials, gentleness in conflict, and perseverance in faith. True virtue is not about outward appearances but a sincere devotion to God and a heart aligned with His will.

Jesus calls us to be the "light of the world" (Matthew 5:14), and our virtues should shine as a testimony to His presence within us. As we grow in Christlikeness, our lives become a reflection of His love, drawing others to Him. Let us strive daily to develop and practice these virtues, allowing them to shape our character and strengthen our witness in a world in need of God's grace.

Day 1 – ἀγάπη (agápē) – Love

Greek Word: ἀγάπη
English Word: Love
Meaning: Selfless, sacrificial love that transcends mere feelings and is demonstrated through actions.
Bible Reference: 1 Corinthians 13:4-7 – "Love is patient, love is

kind..."

Devotional Message:

Love, as expressed in ἀγάπη, is the very heartbeat of the Christian faith. It calls us to extend grace without expecting anything in return and to see others as God sees them. In a world often driven by self-interest, agápē challenges us to embrace a love that is unconditional and transformative. This type of love empowers us to forgive, to serve, and to support those in need, even when it requires personal sacrifice. When we practice agápē, we reflect the heart of our Savior, who demonstrated His love by laying down His life. It reminds us that true love is not fleeting or superficial but enduring and robust, capable of overcoming every obstacle. Embracing agápē compels us to act with compassion and seek the welfare of others above our own desires.

Reflection Questions for the Day:

- How can I demonstrate unconditional love to someone who may not expect it?
- In what ways does agápē challenge my current understanding of love?
- What practical steps can I take today to embody this sacrificial love in my community?

Day 2 – ταπεινοφροσύνη (tapeinophrosýnē) – Humility

Greek Word: ταπεινοφροσύνη
English Word: Humility
Meaning: A modest view of oneself; an acknowledgment of one's limitations and dependence on God.
Bible Reference: Philippians 2:3 – "Do nothing out of selfish ambition or vain conceit..."

Devotional Message:

Humility, or ταπεινοφροσύνη, is the quality that enables us to serve others without seeking our own glory. It involves recognizing that every talent, every achievement, and every blessing is ultimately a gift from God. In practicing humility, we allow God's will to guide our actions, knowing that self-exaltation is not the path to true greatness. This virtue teaches us to listen more and speak less, valuing the opinions and needs of others above our own. Humility opens our hearts to correction and growth, ensuring that pride never takes root. It is in our humble acknowledgment of our limitations that we find the strength to rely on God. By embracing ταπεινοφροσύνη, we mirror the example of Christ, who humbled Himself even unto death.

Reflection Questions for the Day:

- What areas of my life need a greater measure of humility?
- How can I better serve others without seeking recognition?
- In what ways can I remind myself daily that all I have is by God's grace?

Day 3 – πραΰτης (praýtēs) – Gentleness

Greek Word: πραΰτης
English Word: Gentleness
Meaning: A meek and mild disposition characterized by a calm and tender spirit.
Bible Reference: Galatians 5:23 – "But the fruit of the Spirit is love, joy, peace, patience, kindness, goodness, faithfulness..."

Devotional Message:

Gentleness, encapsulated in πραΰτης, is a virtue that calls us to respond with a soft and considerate heart even in challenging situations. It is the gentle touch of a shepherd leading his flock, guiding with care rather than force. This quality does not denote weakness; rather, it is a sign of inner strength and confidence in God's protection. When we are gentle, we offer a listening ear and a compassionate presence that can heal wounds and restore hope. It is a reflection of Christ's own manner, who met harshness with kindness and bitterness with love. Practicing gentleness encourages a peaceful spirit in our lives and the lives of those around us. In embracing πραΰτης, we become instruments of God's peace in a turbulent world.

Reflection Questions for the Day:

- How do I react when faced with conflict, and how can I respond more gently?
- What are some practical ways I can exhibit gentleness in my daily interactions?
- In what ways does practicing gentleness help me reflect the character of Christ?

Day 4 – Ὑπομονή (hypomonḗ) – Patience/Endurance

Greek Word: Ὑπομονή

English Word: Patience/Endurance

Meaning: The steadfast perseverance in the face of trials and delays, trusting in God's timing.

Bible Reference: James 1:3-4 – "because you know that the testing of your faith produces perseverance..."

Devotional Message:

Patience, or Ὑπομονή, is more than simply waiting; it is the active endurance of trials with a steadfast heart. This virtue teaches us to trust that God's timing is perfect, even when we face delays and setbacks. It reminds us that challenges are not dead ends, but opportunities for growth and deepening faith. Through ὑπομονή, we learn to lean not on our own understanding but on the eternal promises of God. It encourages us to hold fast to hope during the storms of life, knowing that our endurance is refined like gold in the fire of adversity. Patience fosters an inner peace that transcends circumstances, enabling us to respond with calm assurance. By cultivating this quality, we develop a resilient spirit that reflects the enduring love of our Savior.

Reflection Questions for the Day:

- When have I struggled with impatience, and how might I better trust God's timing?
- What current challenges in my life require a greater measure of endurance?
- How can I cultivate a spirit of patience in both good times and bad?

Day 5 – δικαιοσύνη (dikaiosýnē) – Righteousness

Greek Word: δικαιοσύνη
English Word: Righteousness
Meaning: Moral uprightness; living in accordance with God's standards and truth.
Bible Reference: Matthew 5:6 – "Blessed are those who hunger and thirst for righteousness..."

Devotional Message:

Righteousness, represented by δικαιοσύνη, calls us to align our lives with God's perfect moral standards. It is not merely a legalistic observance but a deep, heartfelt commitment to doing what is right in the eyes of the Lord. When we pursue righteousness, we seek to honor God in every thought, word, and deed. This pursuit challenges us to examine our motives and to cleanse our hearts from sin. It is a journey that demands constant self-reflection, repentance, and renewal. Through living a life of righteousness, we become beacons of God's truth and love in a fallen world. By striving for δικαιοσύνη, we invite God to transform us into vessels that reflect His glory and mercy.

Reflection Questions for the Day:

- In what ways can I better align my actions with God's standards?
- How do I react when I fall short of righteousness, and what steps can I take to repent?
- What practical changes can I make to become a more effective ambassador of God's truth?

Day 6 – εὐσέβεια (eusebeia) – Godliness

Greek Word: εὐσέβεια
English Word: Godliness
Meaning: A devout reverence for God that permeates every aspect of life.
Bible Reference: 1 Timothy 4:8 – "For physical training is of some value, but godliness has value for all things..."

Devotional Message:

Godliness, or εὐσέβεια, is a deep-rooted respect and reverence for the Almighty that transforms our entire being. It goes beyond mere outward rituals and manifests in a lifestyle of integrity, devotion, and constant communion with God. When we pursue godliness, we honor God with our thoughts, actions, and decisions, making Him the center of our lives. This virtue cultivates a heart that is sensitive to the promptings of the Holy Spirit and aware of the presence of the Divine in every moment. It encourages us to cultivate spiritual disciplines—prayer, meditation on Scripture, and worship—that fortify our faith. Godliness leads us to serve others selflessly and to live in a way that inspires and uplifts those around us. Embracing εὐσέβεια means allowing God to shape our character so that our lives become a living testimony of His love and truth.

Reflection Questions for the Day:

- How can I deepen my relationship with God to reflect genuine godliness?
- What daily habits can I develop to remind myself of God's presence?
- In what ways does my current lifestyle honor or dishonor God?

Day 7 – φιλανθρωπία (philanthrōpía) – Kindness/Love for Humanity

Greek Word: φιλανθρωπία
English Word: Kindness (or Love for Humanity)
Meaning: Compassionate care and concern for others, leading to acts of generosity and support.
Bible Reference: Titus 3:4 – "But when the kindness and love of God our Savior appeared..."

Devotional Message:

Kindness, expressed in φιλανθρωπία, is the outward demonstration of God's love toward humanity. It calls us to be compassionate and empathetic, reaching out to those who are hurting or in need. When we act with kindness, we imitate the heart of our Savior, who showed mercy and compassion to all people. This virtue motivates us to lend a helping hand, to listen attentively, and to encourage those who feel isolated or discouraged. It is not a passive feeling, but an active commitment to make a difference in the lives of others. By practicing φιλανθρωπία, we break down barriers and foster a community of love and acceptance. Our acts of kindness, no matter how small, have the power to transform lives and spread the light of Christ in a dark world.

Reflection Questions for the Day:

- What are some concrete ways I can show kindness to those around me today?
- How does demonstrating φιλανθρωπία help me grow in my faith?
- In what areas of my life can I be more proactive in sharing God's love?

Conclusion – Christian Virtues

Throughout this week, we have journeyed through foundational virtues that shape our identity as followers of Christ. We began with ἀγάπη, a love that is selfless and sacrificial, reminding us that true love is the highest expression of faith. We then explored ταπεινοφροσύνη, which calls us to live with humility and recognize our dependence on God. In practicing πραΰτης, we learned that gentleness can be a powerful force in a world that often values strength over sensitivity. The virtue of ὑπομονή taught us that enduring hardships with patience can lead to spiritual maturity. In our pursuit of δικαιοσύνη, we were reminded of the need to align our lives with God's truth and moral standards. Our reflection on εὐσέβεια deepened our understanding of what it means to live in constant reverence for God, and finally, φιλανθρωπία encouraged us to extend compassion and care to others. Collectively, these virtues build a robust framework for Christian living, inviting us to mirror the character of Christ in every aspect of our lives and to be a beacon of hope and light in our communities.

Week 2 Theme: Spiritual Fruit

Spiritual Fruit: Evidence of a Transformed Life

The fruit of the Spirit is the evidence of God's transformative work in a believer's life. As described in **Galatians 5:22-23**, the Spirit produces love, joy, peace, patience, kindness, goodness, faithfulness, gentleness, and self-control in those who walk with Christ. These qualities are not merely moral virtues but divine characteristics that grow as we surrender to the Holy Spirit's leading.

Spiritual fruit is not achieved by human effort alone but is cultivated through a close relationship with God. Just as a tree must remain rooted to bear fruit, we must abide in Christ (John 15:5). When we stay connected to Him through prayer, worship, and obedience to His Word, His Spirit works within us, refining our character and shaping us into His image.

This fruit is not for personal gain but for the glory of God and the blessing of others. A life marked by the fruit of the Spirit becomes a testimony of God's grace, drawing others to Him. Let us seek to cultivate these qualities daily, allowing the Spirit to work through us so that our lives may reflect the love, joy, and peace that only Christ can give.

Day 8 – χαρά (chará) – Joy

Greek Word: χαρά
English Word: Joy
Meaning: A deep, inner gladness that comes from a secure relationship with God, independent of external circumstances.
Bible Reference: Galatians 5:22 – "But the fruit of the Spirit is love, joy, peace..."

Devotional Message:

Joy (χαρά) is not merely a fleeting emotion but a state of being rooted in the steadfast love and grace of God. It transcends momentary happiness by drawing its strength from our relationship with the Creator. Even in times of hardship or uncertainty, the joy of the Lord becomes a refuge and a sustaining force. This joy fuels our faith, encouraging us to look beyond the temporary and to focus on eternal promises. It is a reminder that our contentment is found not in worldly circumstances but in the everlasting goodness of God. When we allow this divine joy to fill our hearts, we become beacons of light, capable of uplifting those around us. Embracing χαρά transforms our outlook, turning challenges into opportunities for spiritual growth.

Reflection Questions for the Day:

- How can I cultivate a deeper sense of joy that remains steady despite life's challenges?
- In what ways has God's joy impacted my daily attitude?
- How might I share this joy with someone who is struggling today?

Day 9 – εἰρήνη (eirḗnē) – Peace

Greek Word: εἰρήνη

English Word: Peace

Meaning: The inner tranquility and calm assurance that comes from knowing God's presence and sovereignty.

Bible Reference: Galatians 5:22 – "...peace..."

Devotional Message:

Peace (εἰρήνη) is more than the absence of conflict—it is a deep, abiding calm that settles within our hearts when we trust in God. This divine peace anchors us in the midst of life's storms, offering solace and clarity in times of distress. It reminds us that true contentment and safety are found in God's unchanging nature and promises. As we cultivate a peaceful spirit, we learn to let go of anxiety and fear, replacing them with trust and hope. This peace extends beyond personal serenity; it enables us to be instruments of reconciliation in our relationships and communities. By embracing εἰρήνη, we invite God's quiet assurance into every facet of our lives, allowing it to guide our thoughts, words, and actions. Ultimately, this peace becomes a powerful testimony of God's love in a chaotic world.

Reflection Questions for the Day:

- What steps can I take today to welcome God's peace into my heart?
- In which areas of my life do I struggle to experience true peace, and why?
- How can I be a channel of God's peace to those around me?

Day 10 – μακροθυμία (makrothymía) – Long-suffering

Greek Word: μακροθυμία
English Word: Long-suffering
Meaning: The capacity to endure hardship, delays, and provocation with patience and perseverance.
Bible Reference: Galatians 5:22 – "...long-suffering..."

Devotional Message:

Long-suffering (μακροθυμία) invites us to embrace patience as a vital aspect of our spiritual journey. It teaches us to endure trials and setbacks with a calm spirit, recognizing that growth often comes through perseverance. This virtue is not passive; it requires an active trust in God's perfect timing. When we practice μακροθυμία, we learn to wait with hope and remain steadfast even when immediate answers seem absent. It is a gentle reminder that the challenges we face are opportunities for refinement and deeper reliance on the Lord. By cultivating long-suffering, we align our hearts with the character of Christ, who endured the cross for our salvation. Ultimately, this endurance transforms our struggles into stepping stones toward spiritual maturity.

Reflection Questions for the Day:

- How do I react when faced with delays or setbacks in my life?
- What can I learn from God's example of patience in my current trials?
- How might I cultivate a spirit of long-suffering that reflects Christ's endurance?

Day 11 – χρηστότης (chrēstótēs) – Kindness

Greek Word: χρηστότης
English Word: Kindness
Meaning: The quality of being benevolent, compassionate, and considerate toward others.
Bible Reference: Galatians 5:22 – "...kindness..."

Devotional Message:

Kindness (χρηστότης) is a gentle, compassionate virtue that reflects God's heart for humanity. It calls us to act with empathy and generosity, extending care and warmth to those around us. When we embody this quality, we become tangible expressions of God's love in the world. Kindness is often found in the simple acts— a smile, a helping hand, or a word of encouragement—that can brighten someone's day and restore hope. It is not forced or artificial but flows naturally when we allow the Holy Spirit to guide our actions. As we practice χρηστότης, we break down barriers, build bridges, and foster a spirit of community. In this way, our lives become living testimonies of the transforming power of God's love.

Reflection Questions for the Day:

- In what ways can I express kindness to those in my community today?
- How does the act of being kind to others change my perspective on life?
- What are some practical steps I can take to cultivate a heart full of compassion?

Day 12 – ἀγαθωσύνη (agathōsýnē) – Goodness

Greek Word: ἀγαθωσύνη

English Word: Goodness

Meaning: Moral excellence; the innate quality of doing what is right and beneficial for others.

Bible Reference: Galatians 5:22 – "...goodness..."

Devotional Message:

Goodness (ἀγαθωσύνη) calls us to reflect the character of God through our actions and choices. It is the embodiment of moral integrity and an unwavering commitment to what is right. This virtue challenges us to pursue righteousness not for personal gain, but for the benefit of those around us. When we practice goodness, we engage in acts that uplift, encourage, and build up our communities. It is a conscious decision to live out the principles of honesty, fairness, and compassion in every situation. Embracing ἀγαθωσύνη transforms our interactions, making our lives a source of light in a world that desperately needs hope. By aligning ourselves with this quality, we mirror the benevolence of our Savior and contribute to a more just and loving society.

Reflection Questions for the Day:

- How can I actively demonstrate goodness in my daily interactions?
- In what ways does living with moral excellence impact my relationships with others?
- What steps can I take to ensure my actions consistently reflect the goodness of God?

Day 13 – πίστις (pístis) – Faith (Fidelity)

Greek Word: πίστις
English Word: Faith
Meaning: Trust, confidence, and loyalty in God's promises and character.
Bible Reference: Galatians 5:22 – "...faith..."

Devotional Message:

Faith (πίστις) is the cornerstone of our spiritual journey, anchoring us in God's unchanging truth. It goes beyond mere belief; it is an active trust and fidelity that shapes our actions and decisions. When we have true πίστις, we are confident that God is in control, even in the face of uncertainty or adversity. This trust enables us to step out in obedience, knowing that our efforts, however small, are part of a greater divine plan. Faith sustains us through trials, reminding us of the promises that have been spoken over our lives. It nurtures a deep, personal relationship with God and transforms our perspective on life's challenges. By embracing this steadfast faith, we grow stronger in our walk with Christ and become beacons of hope to those around us.

Reflection Questions for the Day:

- How can I strengthen my trust in God during moments of uncertainty?
- In what ways has my faith been tested, and how did I respond?
- How can I actively live out my commitment to God's promises today?

Day 14 – ἐγκράτεια (enkráteia) – Self-control

Greek Word: ἐγκράτεια

English Word: Self-control

Meaning: The ability to master one's impulses, desires, and actions through disciplined faith.

Bible Reference: Galatians 5:23 – "...self-control."

Devotional Message:

Self-control (ἐγκράτεια) is a powerful virtue that allows us to navigate life with discipline and intentionality. It is the ability to restrain impulsive behaviors and to make choices that align with God's will. Practicing self-control helps us resist temptations that may lead us away from our spiritual goals. This quality is essential for personal growth and fosters a life marked by thoughtful actions and deliberate decisions. When we exercise ἐγκράτεια, we create space for the Holy Spirit to guide us, ensuring that our lives reflect the principles of righteousness. It also empowers us to manage our time, resources, and emotions effectively, leading to a balanced and purposeful existence. Embracing self-control transforms our character, enabling us to honor God with every facet of our lives.

Reflection Questions for the Day:

- What areas of my life require greater self-control?
- How can I better align my actions with my long-term spiritual goals?
- What practical habits can I implement to strengthen my discipline and restraint?

Conclusion – Spiritual Fruit

Throughout this week, we have delved into the powerful manifestations of the Spirit that sustain and enrich our lives. We began with χαρά, which reminds us that true joy is a deep, enduring state born of our relationship with God. Next, εἰρήνη taught us that real peace comes from trusting in the sovereignty of the Lord, even amidst life's storms. We learned from μακροθυμία that long-suffering is an active expression of trust in God's perfect timing, while χρηστότης encouraged us to extend kindness in a way that reflects His compassion. Our reflection on ἀγαθωσύνη reminded us that goodness involves living out moral excellence for the benefit of others. The day dedicated to πίστις deepened our understanding of faith as a living, active trust in God's promises. Finally, ἐγκράτεια underscored the importance of self-control in guiding our actions in a way that honors God. Collectively, these virtues form the fruit of the Spirit, providing us with the resources to live out our Christian faith with authenticity and resilience. They challenge us to allow God's work within us to produce a life that is not only pleasing to Him but also a blessing to those around us.

Week 3: Salvation Terms

Salvation: The Gift of Grace Through Christ

Salvation is the greatest gift God has given to humanity—a divine rescue from sin and eternal separation from Him. It is not earned by good works or human effort but is freely given through faith in Jesus Christ. **Ephesians 2:8-9** reminds us, *"For by grace you have been saved through faith, and this is not your own doing; it is the gift of God, not a result of works, so that no one may boast."*

At the heart of salvation is Christ's sacrifice on the cross. Through His death and resurrection, He paid the penalty for our sins and opened the way to eternal life. This gift is available to all who repent, believe in Him, and surrender their lives to His lordship (Romans 10:9). Salvation is not just about securing a place in heaven; it transforms our hearts, renews our minds, and restores our relationship with God.

As recipients of this grace, we are called to live in gratitude, walking in righteousness and sharing the Good News with others. Salvation is both an invitation and a mission—an opportunity to receive God's love and extend it to the world. Today, embrace this gift and let it shape your life forever.

Day 15 – σωτηρία (sōtēría) – Salvation

Greek Word: σωτηρία
English Word: Salvation
Meaning: Deliverance from sin and its consequences through the redemptive work of Christ.
Bible Reference: Romans 10:10 – "For with the heart one believes and is justified, and with the mouth one confesses and is saved."

Devotional Message:

Salvation (σωτηρία) stands at the very heart of the Christian faith, representing God's gracious act of delivering us from sin and death. It is a gift that transforms our lives, freeing us from the chains of guilt and the burden of a fallen nature. When we embrace salvation, we accept not only forgiveness but also the promise of eternal life with our Creator. This profound truth calls us to reflect on the magnitude of God's mercy and the sacrificial love of Christ, who bore our sins on the cross. In our daily walk, remembering our salvation instills hope and courage to face the challenges of life. It reminds us that our identity is not defined by past mistakes but by the redemption we have received through faith. As we meditate on σωτηρία, we are encouraged to share this life-changing message with others, offering them the invitation to experience the same freedom.

Reflection Questions for the Day:

- How has the reality of my salvation transformed my view of my past and my future?
- In what ways can I be a living testimony to the saving grace of God?
- How does the promise of salvation inspire hope and resilience in my daily life?

Day 16 – λύτρον (lýtron) – Ransom

Greek Word: λύτρον
English Word: Ransom
Meaning: The price paid for the liberation of captives, symbolizing Christ's sacrifice to free us from sin.
Bible Reference: Matthew 20:28 – "Just as the Son of Man did not come to be served, but to serve, and to give his life as a ransom for many."

Devotional Message:

The term λύτρον (ransom) paints a vivid picture of redemption by highlighting the costly nature of our freedom. It reminds us that our release from sin was not free—it was purchased with the precious life of Jesus Christ. This imagery challenges us to appreciate the immense sacrifice that set us free and to live in gratitude for the price paid on our behalf. When we reflect on the concept of a ransom, we see how it underscores the seriousness of sin and the extraordinary love of a Savior willing to give everything for our deliverance. It calls us to examine our lives, recognizing that every blessing we enjoy is secured by Christ's sacrifice. This truth also motivates us to value and protect the freedom we have, living in a manner worthy of the ransom that was paid. Embracing λύτρον encourages us to extend compassion and hope to others who remain in spiritual captivity.

Reflection Questions for the Day:

- How does understanding Christ's ransom influence the way I live each day?
- What steps can I take to honor the price that was paid for my freedom?
- In what ways can I share the message of Christ's ransom with someone who feels spiritually captive?

Day 17 – ἀπολύτρωσις (apolýtrōsis) – Redemption

Greek Word: ἀπολύτρωσις

English Word: Redemption

Meaning: The act of being set free from the bondage of sin and its penalties through Christ's sacrifice.

Bible Reference: Ephesians 1:7 — "In him we have redemption through his blood, the forgiveness of sins, in accordance with the riches of God's grace."

Devotional Message:

Redemption (ἀπολύτρωσις) speaks to the transformative power of God's grace that liberates us from the slavery of sin. It is through this redemption that we are restored to a right relationship with God, freed from the consequences of our wrongdoing. The imagery of redemption is rich with hope, illustrating that no matter how deep our sin, the blood of Christ can redeem and renew us. It challenges us to leave behind our past failures and embrace the new life offered in Him. In the process of redemption, we are not only forgiven but also called to live differently—reflecting God's love and grace in every aspect of our lives. This truth instills in us a sense of purpose and an unwavering commitment to walk in the freedom that has been granted. As we celebrate ἀπολύτρωσις, we are reminded to extend the same grace to others, inviting them to experience the redeeming power of Christ.

Reflection Questions for the Day:

- How has the redemption I have received impacted my personal identity?
- In what areas of my life do I still feel bound, and how can I fully embrace the freedom offered in Christ?
- How can I actively demonstrate the redemptive power of God's grace in my interactions with others?

Day 18 – δικαίωσις (dikaíōsis) – Justification

Greek Word: δικαίωσις
English Word: Justification
Meaning: The divine declaration of a believer's righteousness, achieved through faith in Jesus Christ.

Bible Reference: Romans 5:16 – "And the gift is not like the result of one man's sin: The judgment followed one sin and brought condemnation, but the gift followed many trespasses and brought justification."

Devotional Message:

Justification (δικαίωσις) is the act by which God declares us to be righteous, not because of our own works, but solely on the basis of Christ's sacrifice. It is a profound expression of God's mercy that removes the stain of sin from our lives and grants us a new standing before Him. When we are justified, our past misdeeds are no longer held against us; instead, we are clothed in the righteousness of our Savior. This truth liberates us from the burden of self-condemnation and fills us with the assurance of God's unconditional love. It invites us to live confidently in the freedom that comes from being made right with God. Justification also serves as a powerful reminder of the unmerited favor we receive—a favor that calls us to extend grace and forgiveness to others. Embracing δικαίωσις transforms our self-perception and encourages us to pursue lives that reflect the holiness we have received.

Reflection Questions for the Day:

- How does the truth of my justification change the way I view my past mistakes?
- In what ways can I live out the freedom that comes from being declared righteous by God?
- How can I extend the message of justification to those struggling with feelings of guilt and inadequacy?

Day 19 – καταλλαγή (katallagḗ) – Reconciliation

Greek Word: καταλλαγή

English Word: Reconciliation

Meaning: The restoration of a broken relationship, particularly between God and humanity, through Christ's atoning work.

Bible Reference: 2 Corinthians 5:18 – "All this is from God, who reconciled us to himself through Christ and gave us the ministry of reconciliation."

Devotional Message:

Reconciliation (καταλλαγή) represents the healing of the deep rift caused by sin between God and humanity. It is a divine act that brings restoration and mends what was once fractured. Through the sacrifice of Jesus, reconciliation becomes possible, opening the door for a renewed and intimate relationship with our Creator. This powerful concept teaches us that no distance or division is too great to be overcome by God's love. As we experience reconciliation, we are called to be ambassadors of this peace, sharing the good news that God's grace can restore even the most broken relationships. It challenges us to forgive others and seek forgiveness, fostering unity and harmony in our communities. By embracing καταλλαγή, we not only restore our own relationship with God but also become instruments of His healing in the world.

Reflection Questions for the Day:

- How has reconciliation changed my relationship with God and with others?
- In what areas of my life do I need to seek or offer reconciliation?
- How can I actively participate in the ministry of reconciliation that God has entrusted to me?

Day 20 – Ἱλασμός (hilasmós) – Propitiation

Greek Word: ἱλασμός

English Word: Propitiation

Meaning: The act of appeasing God's wrath through a sacrificial offering, thereby restoring His favor toward sinners.

Bible Reference: 1 John 2:2 – "He is the propitiation for our sins, and not for ours only but also for the sins of the whole world."

Devotional Message:

Propitiation (ἱλασμός) reveals the astonishing love of God in His willingness to appease divine wrath through the sacrifice of His Son. It underscores the reality that sin, which separates us from God, demands a penalty that Christ willingly bore on our behalf. This concept invites us to ponder the magnitude of Christ's love and the cost of our redemption. In understanding propitiation, we see that God's justice and mercy are perfectly balanced in the cross, where judgment was met with grace. This sacrificial act not only restores our standing before God but also invites us to live lives marked by gratitude and reverence. It challenges us to never take for granted the depth of God's forgiveness and the price that was paid to secure our salvation. Embracing ἱλασμός calls us to respond with a heart of worship and a commitment to honor the sacrifice of Jesus in all that we do.

Reflection Questions for the Day:

- How does the concept of propitiation deepen my understanding of God's justice and mercy?
- In what ways can I express gratitude for the sacrifice of Christ in my daily life?
- How can I live in a manner that reflects the magnitude of the love that appeased God's wrath on my behalf?

Day 21 – μετάνοια (metánoia) – Repentance

Greek Word: μετάνοια
English Word: Repentance
Meaning: A transformative change of mind and heart that turns one away from sin and toward God.
Bible Reference: Mark 1:15 – "The time is fulfilled, and the kingdom of God is at hand; repent and believe in the gospel."

Devotional Message:

Repentance (μετάνοια) is a life-altering decision that invites us to turn away from our old ways and embrace a new path in Christ. It involves a sincere change of heart and mind—a reorientation of our desires and actions toward God's will. This act of turning away from sin is not just about regret; it is about a heartfelt commitment to transformation and renewal. In repentance, we acknowledge our shortcomings, ask for forgiveness, and seek to align our lives with God's purposes. It is a continual process that requires humility, honesty, and the willingness to let go of past mistakes. As we practice μετάνοια, we experience the liberating power of God's grace that wipes away our sins and gives us a fresh start. This transformative journey draws us closer to our Savior, deepening our relationship with Him and equipping us to extend forgiveness and hope to others.

Reflection Questions for the Day:

- What areas of my life need a sincere turning point toward God?
- How has repentance led to personal growth and renewal in my spiritual journey?
- What steps can I take today to fully embrace the transformative power of μετάνοια?

Conclusion – Salvation Terms

This week, we have journeyed through the profound and multifaceted aspects of salvation as revealed in Scripture. We began with σωτηρία, a reminder of the transformative deliverance that God offers to each believer. The concept of λύτρον challenged us to appreciate the costly sacrifice that set us free from sin's grip.

In exploring ἀπολύτρωσις, we witnessed the redemptive power that restores us to a life of hope and purpose. Our reflection on δικαίωσις reinforced that our righteousness comes solely from faith in Christ, not from our own merits. Through καταλλαγή, we learned about the healing and restoring nature of God's love, which mends broken relationships. The day dedicated to ἱλασμός revealed the awe-inspiring act of appeasing divine wrath through sacrifice, and finally, μετάνοια invited us into a continual process of transformation and renewal. Together, these salvation terms create a rich tapestry that defines the core of the Gospel, urging us to live lives of gratitude, humility, and active witness to the redeeming love of our Savior.

Week 4: Person of Christ.

The Person of Christ: Fully God, Fully Man

Jesus Christ is the central figure of our faith, the perfect revelation of God to humanity. He is both fully God and fully man, embodying divine power and human frailty in a way that no one else ever has. **John 1:14** declares, *"The Word became flesh and dwelt among us, and we have seen his glory, glory as of the only Son from the Father, full of grace and truth."*

As God, Jesus possesses all authority, holiness, and perfection. He existed before creation, spoke the universe into being, and continues to sustain all things by His power (Colossians 1:16-17). As man, He experienced hunger, pain, and sorrow, yet He lived a sinless life, becoming the perfect sacrifice for our sins. His humanity allows Him to sympathize with our weaknesses, while His divinity assures us that He has the power to save.

The person of Christ is the foundation of our salvation, our hope, and our faith. He is the Good Shepherd, the Light of the World, the King of Kings, and our risen Savior. To know Christ is to know God Himself (John 14:9). May we seek Him daily, follow His example, and worship Him as the true and living Lord.

Day 22 – Χριστός (Christós) – Christ / Messiah

Greek Word: Χριστός
English Word: Christ / Messiah
Meaning: The Anointed One; the long-awaited deliverer and savior prophesied in Scripture.
Bible Reference: Matthew 16:16 – "Simon Peter replied, 'You are the Messiah, the Son of the living God.'"

Devotional Message:

Christ (Χριστός) stands as the cornerstone of our faith, representing the fulfillment of Old Testament prophecies and the hope of salvation. He is the Anointed One, chosen and empowered by God to bring redemption to a broken world. In acknowledging Christ as our Messiah, we recognize the divine initiative in our rescue from sin and despair. His life, death, and resurrection exemplify God's unfathomable love and the ultimate triumph over death. As we meditate on Christ's identity, we are reminded that our hope does not rest in human effort but in the divine promise that He will lead us into everlasting life. His example inspires us to live in obedience, love, and humility, reflecting His character in our daily interactions. Embracing the truth of Χριστός calls us to not only trust in His saving work but also to proclaim His name boldly to a world in need.

Reflection Questions for the Day:

- How does acknowledging Christ as the Messiah change the way I view my own life and purpose?
- In what practical ways can I reflect the character of Christ in my daily actions?
- How can I share the transformative message of Christ with those around me?

Day 23 – Ἰησοῦς (Iēsoûs) – Jesus

Greek Word: Ἰησοῦς

English Word: Jesus

Meaning: "The Lord saves"; the personal name of the Savior who came to rescue humanity.

Bible Reference: Matthew 1:21 – "She will bear a son, and you shall call his name Jesus, for he will save his people from their sins."

Devotional Message:

Jesus (Ἰησοῦς) is more than a historical figure—He is the living Savior who continues to offer hope and restoration to all who believe. His name, meaning "The Lord saves," encapsulates the heart of the Gospel, reminding us that our deliverance comes through Him alone. In His earthly ministry, Jesus demonstrated compassion, healed the sick, and brought light to the darkness, revealing God's love in tangible ways. His teachings guide us on how to live a life pleasing to God, while His sacrifice on the cross paves the way for forgiveness and eternal life. Reflecting on Jesus compels us to examine our own lives and surrender our burdens, trusting in His power to redeem and transform. His resurrection assures us of victory over sin and death, inspiring confidence that no trial is insurmountable. By embracing the person of Ἰησοῦς, we are invited into a personal relationship that transforms every facet of our existence.

Reflection Questions for the Day:

- What does the saving work of Jesus mean for me personally?
- How can I draw closer to Jesus in my daily walk with God?
- In what ways can I live out the example of compassion and grace that Jesus modeled?

Day 24 – Ἐμμανουήλ (Emmanouél) – Immanuel

Greek Word: Ἐμμανουήλ

English Word: Immanuel

Meaning: "God with us"; a name that signifies God's intimate presence among His people.

Bible Reference: Matthew 1:23 – "Behold, the virgin shall conceive and bear a son, and they shall call his name Immanuel" (which means, God with us).

Devotional Message:

Immanuel (Ἐμμανουήλ) speaks to the profound reality that God is not distant but has come to dwell among us. This name assures us that in every circumstance, we are never alone because the Creator of the universe is present in our lives. The promise of Immanuel bridges the gap between heaven and earth, offering comfort, guidance, and hope in the midst of life's challenges. His presence transforms our understanding of divine intimacy, inviting us into a relationship where we can experience God's love and care firsthand. As we reflect on Immanuel, we find encouragement to face each day with the confidence that God walks beside us, sharing our joys and burdens. This truth empowers us to live boldly, knowing that our struggles are met with divine support. Embracing Immanuel deepens our faith and reminds us that God's nearness is the ultimate source of strength and peace.

Reflection Questions for the Day:

- How does knowing that God is "with me" change my approach to daily challenges?
- In what ways have I experienced the presence of Immanuel during difficult times?
- How can I cultivate a deeper awareness of God's nearness in my life?

Day 25 – Κύριος (Kýrios) – Lord

Greek Word: Κύριος
English Word: Lord
Meaning: Master, sovereign, and the ultimate authority in the life

of a believer.

Bible Reference: John 20:28 – "Thomas answered him, 'My Lord and my God!'"

Devotional Message:

The title Κύριος (Lord) encapsulates the supreme authority and divine lordship of Jesus over all creation. Recognizing Jesus as Lord means surrendering to His will and acknowledging His rightful place as the ruler of our lives. This declaration is both a confession of faith and an invitation to live under the guidance of divine authority. In submitting to His lordship, we experience the freedom that comes from living in alignment with God's purpose. His authority is not oppressive but liberating, providing order, direction, and peace amid life's chaos. When we call Jesus our Lord, we invite His presence to shape our decisions, priorities, and relationships. Embracing the title Κύριος transforms our hearts and minds, ensuring that our lives are led by the wisdom and truth of God.

Reflection Questions for the Day:

- In what areas of my life do I need to more fully acknowledge Jesus as my Lord?
- How does surrendering to His authority bring order and peace to my daily routine?
- What steps can I take to better align my decisions with the will of my Lord?

Day 26 – ὁδός (hodós) – Way

Greek Word: ὁδός

English Word: Way

Meaning: The path or direction set forth by Christ as the means to salvation and a righteous life.

Bible Reference: John 14:6 – "Jesus said to him, 'I am the way, and the truth, and the life. No one comes to the Father except through me.'"

Devotional Message:

The word ὁδός (Way) represents the unique path of truth and life that Jesus established for His followers. It is a directional call that invites us to leave behind worldly detours and embrace the journey that leads to eternal communion with God. This way is not marked by ease or convenience, but by purpose, discipline, and a reliance on divine guidance. Following the Way means trusting in Jesus as the sole mediator between God and humanity, acknowledging that His teachings light our path in times of darkness. His example and commands serve as our compass, guiding us to live lives marked by integrity and grace. As we commit to walking this Way, we discover that every step brings us closer to the fullness of life promised in the Gospel. Embracing ὁδός challenges us to evaluate our priorities and realign our steps with the eternal plan of God.

Reflection Questions for the Day:

- How do I actively follow the way that Jesus has set for me?
- What obstacles prevent me from walking the full path of righteousness, and how can I overcome them?
- In what ways does following Jesus as the Way bring clarity and purpose to my daily decisions?

Day 27 – λόγος (lógos) – Word

Greek Word: λόγος
English Word: Word
Meaning: The divine communication of God's truth, wisdom, and creative power as revealed in Scripture.

Bible Reference: John 1:1 – "In the beginning was the Word, and the Word was with God, and the Word was God."

Devotional Message:

The term λόγος (Word) encapsulates the living and active message of God, which brings revelation and transformation to our lives. It is through the Word that God communicates His eternal truth, guiding us in faith and illuminating the mysteries of creation. The Word is not a static text but a dynamic force that speaks directly to our hearts, challenging us to grow in wisdom and righteousness. In encountering the Word, we encounter the character of God Himself, whose truth remains unchanging amidst the flux of life. As we immerse ourselves in Scripture, we are invited to let the Word dwell richly in us, transforming our minds and renewing our spirits. It serves as a constant reminder that God's promises are reliable and that His guidance is our sure foundation. Embracing the λόγος in our daily lives equips us to navigate the challenges of the world with confidence and purpose.

Reflection Questions for the Day:

- How does engaging with the Word of God impact my daily life?
- In what ways can I make the study of Scripture a more integral part of my routine?
- How can I allow the truth of the Word to shape my decisions and relationships?

Day 28 – Μεσσίας (Messías) – Messiah

Greek Word: Μεσσίας
English Word: Messiah
Meaning: The anointed one, foretold by the prophets, who fulfills God's promise of salvation and restoration.

Bible Reference: John 1:41 – "He first found his own brother Simon and said to him, 'We have found the Messiah'."

Devotional Message:

The title Μεσσίας (Messiah) emphasizes the fulfillment of ancient prophecies through the coming of Jesus Christ. It highlights that He is the long-awaited deliverer who has been anointed by God to bring salvation, hope, and restoration to a fallen world. Recognizing Jesus as the Messiah calls us to embrace the certainty that God's promises are realized in Him. His arrival marks the turning point in history, where divine purpose and human need meet in perfect harmony. The Messiah's mission is not only to redeem us from sin but also to restore our relationship with God, transforming our hearts and lives. As we reflect on the significance of the Messiah, we are challenged to live in the light of His truth and to be ambassadors of the hope He brings. Embracing Μεσσίας invites us into a journey of faith that redefines our identity and purpose in the world.

Reflection Questions for the Day:

- What does the fulfillment of the Messiah's promise mean for my personal faith journey?
- How can I actively live out the hope and restoration that the Messiah brings?
- In what ways can I share the message of the Messiah with those who have not yet experienced His saving grace?

Conclusion – Person of Christ

Throughout this week, we have delved into the rich and multifaceted identity of Christ as revealed by the original Greek words of the New Testament. We began by affirming His divine appointment as Χριστός, the Anointed One, whose sacrifice brings redemption and hope. We then explored the personal name Ἰησοῦς, a constant reminder of the Savior who offers deliverance to every believer. The name Ἐμμανουήλ reassured us that God is ever-present, walking alongside us in every season of life. Declaring Jesus as Κύριος underscores His rightful authority over our lives, while embracing ὁδός invites us to follow the unique path that leads to eternal life. The revelation of λόγος reminds us of the power of God's Word to transform our hearts and minds, and finally, recognizing Him as Μεσσίας confirms the fulfillment of God's promises in our midst. Together, these devotional messages paint a portrait of a Savior who is both transcendent and intimately involved in our lives—a true Lord, a compassionate guide, and the eternal hope of every soul.

Week 5: Holy Spirit.

The Holy Spirit: Our Helper and Guide

The Holy Spirit is the active presence of God in the life of every believer, empowering, guiding, and transforming us to live according to His will. Jesus promised His disciples in **John 14:16-17**, *"And I will ask the Father, and he will give you another Helper, to be with you forever, even the Spirit of truth..."* This promise is fulfilled in every believer, as the Holy Spirit dwells within us, equipping us to walk in faith and obedience.

The Holy Spirit convicts the world of sin, leads us into all truth, and strengthens us to live out God's calling. He is our Comforter in times of distress, our Teacher who reveals the deep things of God, and our Source of spiritual power. Through Him, we bear the fruit of the Spirit—love, joy, peace, patience, kindness, goodness, faithfulness, gentleness, and self-control (Galatians 5:22-23).

The Spirit also equips us with spiritual gifts for ministry, uniting the Church as one body in Christ. He is not distant or abstract but is present and active in our lives every day. As we surrender to His leading, we experience transformation, deeper intimacy with God, and boldness to share His love with the world.

Day 29 – Πνεῦμα Ἅγιον (Pneûma Hágion) – Holy Spirit

Greek Word: Πνεῦμα Ἅγιον

English Word: Holy Spirit

Meaning: The presence of God's power and love that dwells within believers, guiding, empowering, and comforting them.

Bible Reference: Acts 1:8 – "But you will receive power when the Holy Spirit has come upon you..."

Devotional Message:

The Holy Spirit, or Πνεῦμα Ἅγιον, is the very breath of God, given to us as a gift to empower our lives and transform our hearts. When we receive the Holy Spirit, we are not left to navigate life on our own; instead, we are enabled by divine power to overcome obstacles and to bear witness to God's love. This presence is not abstract but a personal guide who leads, comforts, and convicts us of truth. In moments of uncertainty or weakness, the Holy Spirit becomes our strength and our counselor, drawing us closer to the heart of God. The transformative work of the Spirit brings renewal, igniting our passion for worship and service. As we open our lives to this divine presence, we begin to experience a deep inner peace and a renewed sense of purpose. Embracing the Holy Spirit invites us into an ongoing, intimate relationship with God, where every breath is a reminder of His abiding presence.

Reflection Questions for the Day:

- How have I experienced the presence of the Holy Spirit in my life?
- In what ways does the Holy Spirit guide my decisions and actions each day?
- How can I become more receptive to the gentle promptings of God's Spirit?

Day 30 – παράκλητος (paráklētos) – Helper/Advocate

Greek Word: παράκλητος
English Word: Helper/Advocate
Meaning: A counselor and comforter, one who comes alongside to support and intercede on our behalf.
Bible Reference: John 14:16 – "And I will ask the Father, and he will give you another Helper, to be with you forever."

Devotional Message:

The term παράκλητος, meaning Helper or Advocate, reflects the compassionate role of the Holy Spirit in our lives. As our divine counselor, the Spirit stands ready to comfort us in times of distress, intercede on our behalf, and provide wisdom when we face difficult decisions. This comforting presence reassures us that we are never alone, regardless of the challenges that come our way. The Advocate not only consoles but also empowers us to stand firm in our faith and to live courageously according to God's word. In moments of doubt or fear, the Spirit's help is a constant reminder that God's love is actively working to support and guide us. By inviting the Helper into every area of our lives, we open ourselves to the transformative power of divine wisdom and peace. Embracing παράκλητος enriches our spiritual journey, assuring us that God's compassionate presence is always near.

Reflection Questions for the Day:

- When have I experienced the comfort and guidance of the Holy Spirit as my Helper?
- In what areas of my life do I need the Advocate's support right now?
- How can I better rely on the Holy Spirit for wisdom during times of uncertainty?

Day 31 – ἔλαιον (élaion) – Oil

Greek Word: ἔλαιον

English Word: Oil

Meaning: A symbol of anointing and healing, representing the outpouring of the Holy Spirit's power in our lives.

Bible Reference: James 5:14 – "Is anyone among you sick? Let him call for the elders of the church, and let them pray over him, anointing him with oil in the name of the Lord."

Devotional Message:

The word ἔλαιον, meaning oil, is rich in symbolism, evoking the anointing and healing presence of the Holy Spirit. Just as oil was used in ancient times to consecrate and heal, so too does the Holy Spirit anoint us for service and restoration. This anointing signifies a divine empowerment that sets us apart for God's purposes, marking us as vessels of His grace and mercy. When we experience the anointing of the Spirit, we are reminded of His healing touch that brings restoration to our bodies, minds, and souls. The symbolism of oil also calls us to be agents of healing and comfort to others, extending the care we have received from God. By embracing the power of ἔλαιον, we are encouraged to be proactive in ministering to those in need, demonstrating God's love through acts of compassion. Ultimately, this divine oil refreshes our spirits and reminds us of the continual presence of God's healing power in our lives.

Reflection Questions for the Day:

- How have I experienced the healing and anointing of the Holy Spirit in my life?
- In what ways can I serve as a conduit of God's healing and comfort to others?
- What practical steps can I take to invite the refreshing power of the Holy Spirit into my daily routine?

Day 32 – βαπτίζω ἐν πνεύματι (baptízō en pneumati) – Baptize in the Spirit

Greek Word: βαπτίζω ἐν πνεύματι

English Word: Baptize in the Spirit

Meaning: The act of being immersed in the power and presence of the Holy Spirit, symbolizing a deeper union with God.

Bible Reference: Acts 1:5 – "For John baptized with water, but you will be baptized with the Holy Spirit not many days from now."

Devotional Message:

Baptism in the Spirit, expressed as βαπτίζω ἐν πνεύματι, signifies a profound encounter with the Holy Spirit that transcends the physical act of water baptism. It represents an immersion into the very power and presence of God, inviting us into a deeper, transformative relationship with Him. This spiritual baptism renews our hearts and minds, empowering us to live out our faith with boldness and clarity. As we experience this baptism, we are filled with divine assurance and equipped to bear witness to the Gospel with unwavering conviction. The act reminds us that our identity is continually renewed through the Holy Spirit's work, aligning us with God's purpose for our lives. It also serves as a call to step out of our comfort zones and actively participate in the mission God has given us. Embracing baptism in the Spirit deepens our connection to God and ignites a passion for service and transformation in our community.

Reflection Questions for the Day:

- How have I experienced a deeper union with God through the baptism in the Spirit?
- In what ways does being baptized in the Spirit empower me to serve others more effectively?
- What changes do I notice in my life when I fully yield to the presence of the Holy Spirit?

Day 33 – χαρίσμα (charísma) – Gift

Greek Word: χαρίσμα
English Word: Gift
Meaning: A spiritual endowment given by the Holy Spirit for the edification of the church and the glory of God.
Bible Reference: 1 Corinthians 12:4 – "Now there are varieties of gifts, but the same Spirit…"

Devotional Message:

The concept of χαρίσμα, or Gift, reflects the unique and diverse spiritual abilities bestowed upon believers by the Holy Spirit. Each gift is a manifestation of God's grace, meant to build up the body of Christ and to serve the greater good of His kingdom. These gifts are not for personal pride or gain but are intended to foster unity, compassion, and growth within the community of believers. When we recognize and embrace our spiritual gifts, we become active participants in God's redemptive plan, contributing our unique strengths to His work. The diversity of gifts reminds us that every member of the church has a vital role to play, regardless of the scale of their contribution. As we celebrate these divine endowments, we are encouraged to seek the guidance of the Holy Spirit in discovering and nurturing our own gifts. Embracing χαρίσμα challenges us to serve selflessly and to utilize our talents for the glory of God and the benefit of others.

Reflection Questions for the Day:

- What spiritual gifts has the Holy Spirit given me, and how can I use them to serve others?
- How do I recognize and celebrate the diverse gifts within my community?
- In what ways can I foster an environment that encourages the development of spiritual gifts for the glory of God?

Day 34 – πνευματικός (pneumatikós) – Spiritual

Greek Word: πνευματικός
English Word: Spiritual
Meaning: Pertaining to the inner life and the influence of the Holy Spirit, as opposed to the natural or carnal.
Bible Reference: 1 Corinthians 2:15 – "The spiritual person judges all things, but is himself to be judged by no one."

Devotional Message:

The adjective πνευματικός, meaning Spiritual, invites us to examine the inner dimensions of our lives beyond the physical and material. It challenges us to develop a sensitivity to the movements of the Holy Spirit, discerning the eternal truths that guide our actions and decisions. Living a spiritual life involves prioritizing our relationship with God, cultivating habits of prayer, meditation, and worship. As we grow in spiritual maturity, we begin to see the world through the lens of divine wisdom rather than mere human reasoning. This spiritual discernment empowers us to navigate challenges with grace and to offer thoughtful insight into the complexities of life. Embracing a πνευματικός mindset means allowing the Holy Spirit to transform our thoughts, leading us to live with integrity and purpose. Ultimately, living spiritually enriches our journey, grounding us in the eternal and preparing us for the fullness of God's promise.

Reflection Questions for the Day:

- In what ways can I cultivate a deeper, more spiritual perspective in my daily life?
- How does focusing on my inner spiritual life influence my interactions with the world around me?
- What practices can I adopt to remain sensitive to the guidance of the Holy Spirit throughout the day?

Day 35 – καρπὸς τοῦ πνεύματος (karpòs toû pneúmatos) – Fruit of the Spirit

Greek Word: καρπὸς τοῦ πνεύματος
English Word: Fruit of the Spirit
Meaning: The visible attributes and character traits that manifest in the life of a believer as a result of the Holy Spirit's work, including love, joy, peace, and more.
Bible Reference: Galatians 5:22 – "But the fruit of the Spirit is love, joy, peace, patience, kindness, goodness, faithfulness…"

Devotional Message:

The term καρπὸς τοῦ πνεύματος, or Fruit of the Spirit, encapsulates the transformative evidence of the Holy Spirit's presence in our lives. Unlike spiritual gifts that are given for ministry, the fruit of the Spirit reflects the everyday character of a life surrendered to God. As we grow in our relationship with the Holy Spirit, these qualities—love, joy, peace, patience, kindness, goodness, faithfulness, gentleness, and self-control—become increasingly evident in our behavior. This fruit is the natural outcome of a heart that is fully attuned to the divine, serving as a testimony of God's work within us. It calls us to live in a way that not only blesses our own lives but also radiates hope and encouragement to those around us. Embracing the fruit of the Spirit is a continual process of growth and sanctification, where our actions mirror the character of Christ. In living out these virtues, we become living examples of God's transforming grace in a broken world.

Reflection Questions for the Day:

- Which aspects of the fruit of the Spirit are most evident in my life, and which areas need further growth?
- How can I intentionally cultivate these spiritual attributes in my daily interactions?
- In what ways does bearing the fruit of the Spirit impact those around me, and how can I encourage others in their spiritual journey?

Conclusion – Holy Spirit

Throughout this week, we have journeyed into the heart of the Holy Spirit's work and presence in our lives. We began by embracing the transformative power of the Holy Spirit (Πνεῦμα Ἅγιον) who equips and empowers us to live victoriously. We then learned about the comforting role of the Helper (παράκλητος), who stands beside us in every trial. The symbol of oil (ἔλαιον) reminded us of the anointing and healing that flows from God's presence. We explored the significance of being baptized in the Spirit (βαπτίζω ἐν πνεύματι), deepening our union with God, and recognized the unique spiritual gifts (χάρισμα) that contribute to the edification of the church. Living a πνευματικός life encourages us to focus on our inner spiritual growth and to be sensitive to the Holy Spirit's guidance. Finally, the visible manifestations of the Spirit's work— the fruit (καρπὸς τοῦ πνεύματος)—challenge us to reflect Christ's character in our everyday lives. Together, these truths paint a comprehensive picture of how the Holy Spirit actively shapes our character, directs our steps, and empowers us to be a living testament of God's grace and love.

Week 6: Kingdom of God.

The Kingdom of God: A Present Reality and Future Hope

The Kingdom of God is the divine rule of God over all creation, both in heaven and on earth. Jesus proclaimed, *"The time is fulfilled, and the kingdom of God is at hand; repent and believe in the gospel"* (**Mark 1:15**). His coming signified the arrival of this kingdom, yet its full realization is still to come when Christ returns in glory.

The Kingdom of God is not defined by earthly power or political rule but by righteousness, peace, and joy in the Holy Spirit (Romans 14:17). It is a kingdom where love triumphs over hatred, grace over sin, and life over death. As believers, we are called to seek first the Kingdom of God (Matthew 6:33), living as citizens of heaven while still on earth. This means aligning our lives with God's will, demonstrating His love, and spreading His truth.

Through Christ, we are invited to participate in His Kingdom now—bringing light to the darkness, serving the needy, and sharing the Gospel. One day, this Kingdom will be fully revealed, and God's perfect reign will be established forever. Until then, we live with the hope and expectation of His glorious return.

Day 36 – βασιλεία (basileía) – Kingdom

Greek Word: βασιλεία
English Word: Kingdom
Meaning: The reign or rule of God, where His authority and righteousness prevail.
Bible Reference: Matthew 6:33 – "But seek first his kingdom and his righteousness, and all these things will be given to you as well."

Devotional Message:

The term βασιλεία, or Kingdom, invites us to understand that God's rule is not confined by human boundaries but is a spiritual realm marked by divine order, justice, and love. It calls us to reorient our lives so that God's priorities take precedence over worldly pursuits. As we seek the Kingdom, we are reminded that our citizenship is not of this earth but of a realm where eternal truths prevail. This pursuit transforms our daily decisions, influencing how we interact with others and approach challenges. Living with a Kingdom mindset means aligning our values with God's truth and expecting His provision in every area of our lives. It encourages us to trust in His sovereign power and to live in hope of His promised reign. Embracing the concept of the Kingdom challenges us to become ambassadors of God's rule, bringing His light into the darkness of our world.

Reflection Questions for the Day:

- How do I prioritize God's Kingdom in my daily life?
- In what ways can I reflect the values of God's Kingdom in my relationships and decisions?
- What steps can I take to further align my heart with the rule and righteousness of God?

Day 37 – εὐαγγέλιον τῆς βασιλείας (euangélion tēs basileías) – Gospel of the Kingdom

Greek Word: εὐαγγέλιον τῆς βασιλείας

English Word: Gospel of the Kingdom

Meaning: The good news announcing God's reign, inviting people to repent and enter His rule.

Bible Reference: Matthew 24:14 – "And this gospel of the kingdom will be preached in the whole world as a testimony to all nations, and then the end will come."

Devotional Message:

The Gospel of the Kingdom is the joyous proclamation of God's sovereign rule and the invitation to experience His transformative power. It is a message that calls for repentance, not as a mere apology, but as a turning of the heart toward God's ways. When we embrace this gospel, we recognize that God's reign brings hope, healing, and restoration to a broken world. The good news challenges us to share the transformative message of God's rule with others, becoming bearers of His light in our communities. It is a reminder that the message of the Kingdom is both a present reality and a future hope, inviting all to partake in its blessings. As we meditate on the Gospel of the Kingdom, we are inspired to live with boldness and conviction, knowing that our lives are a testimony to God's eternal promise. This message compels us to be active participants in spreading the hope of Christ's reign across the world.

Reflection Questions for the Day:

- How has the Gospel of the Kingdom transformed my understanding of God's rule?
- In what practical ways can I share this good news with those around me?
- What changes in my life reflect a heart that has embraced the message of the Kingdom?

Day 38 – μετάνοια εἰς τὴν βασιλείαν (metánoia eis tēn basileían) – Repentance unto the Kingdom

Greek Word: μετάνοια εἰς τὴν βασιλείαν
English Word: Repentance unto the Kingdom
Meaning: A heartfelt turning away from sin and a deliberate choice

to align one's life with the principles of God's Kingdom.

Bible Reference: Matthew 4:17 – "From that time Jesus began to preach, saying, 'Repent, for the kingdom of heaven is at hand.'"

Devotional Message:

Repentance unto the Kingdom goes beyond a simple change of mind; it is a transformative decision to leave behind old patterns and to embrace the new life offered by God's reign. This call to repentance is a key element of the Gospel, inviting us to realign our lives with God's perfect will. It involves acknowledging our shortcomings, seeking forgiveness, and making a conscious commitment to live in a manner that reflects Kingdom values. Through repentance, we experience the liberating power of God's grace, which cleanses us from sin and renews our spirit. This turning of the heart is both a personal and communal act, as it invites others into the journey of transformation under God's authority. As we commit to a life of repentance, we grow in humility and reliance on God's mercy, becoming true citizens of His Kingdom. Embracing this call prepares us to live with a renewed purpose and to manifest the light of God in every aspect of our lives.

Reflection Questions for the Day:

- What areas of my life need a sincere turning away from sin?
- How can I more fully embrace the call to repentance and align my actions with Kingdom values?
- In what ways does a lifestyle of repentance deepen my relationship with God and others?

Day 39 – υἱοὶ τῆς βασιλείας (huioì tēs basileías) – Sons of the Kingdom

Greek Word: υἱοὶ τῆς βασιλείας

English Word: Sons of the Kingdom
Meaning: Believers who are adopted into God's family, sharing in the privileges and responsibilities of His reign.
Bible Reference: Matthew 13:38 – "The field is the world, and the good seed stands for the sons of the kingdom."

Devotional Message:

Being called sons of the Kingdom signifies our adopted status as children of God, with all the rights and responsibilities that come with that relationship. It is a reminder that our identity is rooted in our connection to the divine family rather than in our worldly achievements. As sons of the Kingdom, we are invited to live out a life marked by integrity, honor, and commitment to God's purposes. This relationship is one of intimacy, where we experience the love, guidance, and protection of our Heavenly Father. It empowers us to act with confidence and to approach life's challenges with the assurance of divine support. Embracing this identity calls us to be ambassadors of God's love and messengers of His truth, sharing the blessings of the Kingdom with the world. It challenges us to live in a way that reflects our inheritance as God's beloved children and to honor the responsibilities that come with such a treasured relationship.

Reflection Questions for the Day:

- How does understanding my identity as a son of the Kingdom influence my daily decisions?
- In what ways can I live out the responsibilities and privileges of being part of God's family?
- How can I demonstrate to others the love and acceptance that come from belonging to God's Kingdom?

Day 40 – κληρονόμοι βασιλείας (klēronómoi basileías)

– Heirs of the Kingdom

Greek Word: κληρονόμοι βασιλείας
English Word: Heirs of the Kingdom
Meaning: Those who inherit the promises of God's reign, sharing in the eternal blessings and responsibilities of His Kingdom.
Bible Reference: James 2:5 – "Listen, my beloved brothers, has not God chosen those who are poor in the world to be rich in faith and heirs of the kingdom?"

Devotional Message:

To be heirs of the Kingdom is to be granted an inheritance that far surpasses earthly wealth—a promise of eternal blessings, peace, and joy in God's everlasting reign. This inheritance is secured not by our merits, but by God's gracious plan of salvation through Jesus Christ. It calls us to live with a perspective that values eternal rewards over temporary gains, and to invest in what is truly lasting. As heirs, we are entrusted with the responsibility to steward God's gifts wisely, sharing His love and truth with those around us. This identity transforms our priorities, encouraging us to live in a way that reflects the rich legacy of God's promises. It serves as a constant reminder that our struggles and sacrifices in this life have a divine purpose and a heavenly reward. Embracing our status as heirs of the Kingdom empowers us to live boldly, motivated by the hope of the eternal inheritance that awaits us.

Reflection Questions for the Day:

- How does the promise of being an heir of the Kingdom shape my priorities and decisions?
- In what ways can I better steward the gifts and responsibilities entrusted to me as a child of God?
- How can I share the hope of my heavenly inheritance with those facing discouragement?

Day 41 – δικαιοσύνη τῆς βασιλείας (dikaiosýnē tēs basileías) – Righteousness of the Kingdom

Greek Word: δικαιοσύνη τῆς βασιλείας
English Word: Righteousness of the Kingdom
Meaning: The moral and ethical standard established by God's rule, which guides the behavior of His citizens.
Bible Reference: Romans 14:17 – "For the kingdom of God is not a matter of eating and drinking but of righteousness, peace, and joy in the Holy Spirit."

Devotional Message:

The righteousness of the Kingdom represents the pure, unchanging standard of moral excellence that God has established for His people. It is not earned through human effort but is a gift that comes through faith in Jesus Christ. This divine righteousness calls us to live in a manner that reflects God's character—marked by integrity, justice, and compassion. It challenges us to examine our lives, ensuring that our actions align with the truth and values of God's Kingdom. When we pursue this righteousness, we are not only blessed with inner peace and joy but also become beacons of light in a world often shadowed by moral decay. Embracing the righteousness of the Kingdom means rejecting the fleeting standards of the world and committing ourselves to a higher, eternal purpose. It transforms our relationships and guides our decisions, empowering us to be true ambassadors of God's reign.

Reflection Questions for the Day:

- In what areas of my life do I need to pursue greater righteousness that reflects the Kingdom of God?
- How can I better align my actions with the moral and ethical standards of God's Kingdom?

- What practical steps can I take to be a more effective ambassador of the righteousness that comes from Christ?

Day 42 – δύναμις βασιλείας (dýnamis basileías) – Power of the Kingdom

Greek Word: δύναμις βασιλείας
English Word: Power of the Kingdom
Meaning: The dynamic, transformative strength inherent in God's reign, enabling believers to overcome challenges and impact the world.
Bible Reference: 1 Corinthians 4:20 – "For the kingdom of God is not a matter of talk but of power."

Devotional Message:

The power of the Kingdom, δύναμις βασιλείας, is the active, dynamic force that brings God's promises to life in our daily experience. It is not a passive concept but a transformative strength that empowers us to overcome obstacles and to witness the miracles of God at work in our lives. This power is made available to us through the Holy Spirit, enabling us to step out in faith and accomplish things beyond our human abilities. When we tap into the power of the Kingdom, we experience a shift in perspective, realizing that our limitations are overcome by God's limitless strength. It inspires confidence to face trials and to boldly proclaim the Gospel, knowing that God's power works in and through us. Embracing this power calls us to act in faith, to be agents of change, and to live out the dynamic reality of God's reign. It reminds us that the true essence of the Kingdom is not merely theoretical, but a practical, potent force that can transform lives and communities.

Reflection Questions for the Day:

- How have I experienced the power of God's Kingdom in overcoming personal challenges?
- In what ways can I more fully rely on God's dynamic strength in my daily endeavors?
- How can I be a conduit for the power of the Kingdom to bring change to my community?

Conclusion – Kingdom of God

Throughout this week, we have journeyed through the multifaceted aspects of the Kingdom of God, discovering both its promise and its practical implications in our lives. We began by understanding the very nature of God's reign (βασιλεία) and the call to prioritize His rule above all else. The Gospel of the Kingdom (εὐαγγέλιον τῆς βασιλείας) and the call to repentance (μετάνοια εἰς τὴν βασιλείαν) invite us to actively participate in the transformative work of God's rule on earth. As sons (υἱοὶ τῆς βασιλείας) and heirs (κληρονόμοι βασιλείας) of this Kingdom, we are granted a new identity and an eternal inheritance that shapes our daily decisions. The righteousness of the Kingdom (δικαιοσύνη τῆς βασιλείας) calls us to live by a standard that reflects God's perfect character, while the power of the Kingdom (δύναμις βασιλείας) equips us to overcome obstacles and make a lasting impact in the world. Together, these truths challenge us to live as citizens of an eternal Kingdom, bearing witness to God's love, justice, and transformative strength. May the insights from this week inspire us to pursue a deeper, more authentic Kingdom lifestyle, and may our lives reflect the hope and power of God's everlasting reign.

Week 7: The Church.

The Church: The Body of Christ

The Church is not just a building or an institution—it is the living body of Christ, made up of believers from every nation, tribe, and tongue. **Ephesians 1:22-23** declares, *"And He put all things under His feet and gave Him as head over all things to the church, which is His body, the fullness of Him who fills all in all."* As Christ's body, the Church is called to reflect His love, proclaim His truth, and carry out His mission on earth.

The Church exists to worship God, nurture believers, and reach the lost. It is a family of faith, where we encourage, serve, and grow together in unity. The Holy Spirit equips the Church with spiritual gifts to build one another up and fulfill God's work in the world (1 Corinthians 12:12-14). Though diverse in background and abilities, we are united in Christ, striving to live as His hands and feet.

As members of His Church, we are not spectators but active participants in God's Kingdom. We are called to love one another, make disciples, and shine His light. May we embrace our role in His Church, walking in faith, love, and obedience to His calling.

Day 43 – ἐκκλησία (ekklēsía) – Church

Greek Word: ἐκκλησία

English Word: Church

Meaning: The assembly or community of believers called out to follow Christ and live as His body on earth.

Bible Reference: Matthew 16:18 – "And I tell you, you are Peter, and on this rock I will build my church, and the gates of Hades will not prevail against it."

Devotional Message:

The term ἐκκλησία signifies more than a physical building—it represents the living, breathing community of believers united in Christ. As the Church, we are called out from the world to gather as a family of faith, supporting one another in our spiritual journey. This community is built on the foundation of Jesus' teachings and His sacrificial love, providing a refuge and a source of strength in times of need. In the Church, each member contributes uniquely, and together we form the body of Christ that works in harmony for His glory. The ἐκκλησία stands as a testimony to the transformative power of the Gospel, where grace abounds and lives are renewed. It challenges us to seek unity, to care for one another, and to be a light in the midst of a broken world. Embracing our identity as members of the Church calls us to participate actively in the mission of spreading hope and truth.

Reflection Questions for the Day:

- How do I contribute to the unity and mission of the Church in my community?
- In what ways can I deepen my connection with fellow believers?
- How does understanding the Church as a living community shape my faith and daily walk with Christ?

Day 44 – πρεσβύτερος (presbýteros) – Elder

Greek Word: πρεσβύτερος
English Word: Elder
Meaning: A mature and respected leader within the Church who provides spiritual guidance and wisdom.
Bible Reference: 1 Timothy 5:17 – "The elders who direct the affairs of the church well are worthy of double honor, especially

those whose work is preaching and teaching."

Devotional Message:

The role of the πρεσβύτερος, or elder, is a vital part of the Church's leadership, providing wisdom, care, and direction to the flock of believers. Elders are called to lead by example, demonstrating maturity in faith, integrity, and humility. Their guidance helps nurture the spiritual growth of the community, ensuring that the truth of the Gospel is preserved and passed on to future generations. In their counsel, we find comfort and assurance, knowing that their experience and dedication point us toward Christ. The presence of elders in the Church emphasizes the importance of mentorship, accountability, and intergenerational connection. Their leadership is both a blessing and a responsibility, as they model the character of Christ in serving others selflessly. Embracing the value of elder leadership inspires all believers to grow in wisdom and to support one another in the pursuit of godliness.

Reflection Questions for the Day:

- How can I learn from and honor the spiritual wisdom of the elders in my church?
- What qualities of mature leadership do I see reflected in their example?
- How might I contribute to fostering an environment of mentorship and accountability within the community?

Day 45 – ἐπίσκοπος (epískopos) – Overseer/Bishop

Greek Word: ἐπίσκοπος
English Word: Overseer/Bishop
Meaning: A leader responsible for shepherding the Church,

ensuring spiritual oversight, teaching, and care for the congregation.

Bible Reference: Titus 1:7 – "For an overseer, as God's steward, must be above reproach, faithful to his wife, a man whose children believe and are not open to the charge of debauchery or insubordination."

Devotional Message:

The ἐπίσκοπος, or overseer, holds a position of profound responsibility, acting as a shepherd who tends to the spiritual well-being of the Church. This role demands a heart of service, one that prioritizes the needs of the flock and provides guidance anchored in the truth of Scripture. Overseers are tasked with nurturing the growth of the community, addressing challenges, and maintaining the integrity of the faith. Their leadership is marked by humility, diligence, and a deep commitment to the principles of Christ's teachings. By overseeing the spiritual welfare of the Church, they help create an environment where every believer can flourish. Their example challenges us to value disciplined, servant-hearted leadership in our own lives. Embracing the concept of an overseer reminds us that true authority in the Church is expressed through care, accountability, and love for God's people.

Reflection Questions for the Day:

- What qualities do I admire in the overseers of my church, and how can I emulate them?
- How does strong spiritual oversight contribute to the health of our community?
- In what ways can I support and honor those who serve in leadership within the Church?

Day 46 – διάκονος (diákonos) – Deacon

Greek Word: διάκονος

English Word: Deacon

Meaning: A servant leader within the Church, responsible for practical acts of service and ministering to the needs of the congregation.

Bible Reference: 1 Timothy 3:8 – "Deacons likewise must be dignified, not double-tongued, not addicted to much wine, not greedy for dishonest gain."

Devotional Message:

The term διάκονος signifies a servant leadership role within the Church, where acts of service and compassion are at the forefront of ministry. Deacons are the hands and feet of the Church, addressing practical needs and demonstrating the love of Christ through tangible actions. Their service is a reflection of Christ's example, characterized by humility, integrity, and selflessness. By ministering to the needs of others, deacons help to create a community where every member feels valued and cared for. Their work often goes unnoticed, yet it is critical to the smooth functioning and nurturing of the Church. The role of a deacon challenges each believer to be actively engaged in acts of kindness and support, ensuring that no one is left behind. Embracing the spirit of diakonship calls us to look for opportunities to serve others, reflecting the compassionate heart of our Savior.

Reflection Questions for the Day:

- How can I cultivate a servant's heart in my daily interactions?
- In what practical ways can I serve my church and community as an expression of my faith?
- How does the example of deacons inspire me to look beyond my own needs and reach out to others?

Day 47 – οἰκοδομή (oikodomḗ) – Edification

Greek Word: οἰκοδομή

English Word: Edification

Meaning: The building up or strengthening of the Church through teaching, encouragement, and mutual support.

Bible Reference: 1 Corinthians 14:26 – "What then, brothers? When you come together, each one has a hymn, a lesson, a revelation, a tongue, or an interpretation. Let all things be done for building up (οἰκοδομή)."

Devotional Message:

Οἰκοδομή, or edification, is the process by which the Church grows in strength, maturity, and unity through mutual encouragement and teaching. This concept is central to the life of the community, as every believer is called to contribute to the spiritual growth of others. Edification involves both the impartation of wisdom through the Word of God and the practical support we offer one another in times of need. It is a continuous process of building up the body of Christ, ensuring that each member is equipped to fulfill their God-given purpose. As we engage in edifying one another, we create an environment where faith is nurtured, and doubts are addressed with compassion and clarity. This collaborative effort strengthens the Church and reinforces the bonds of love and unity among believers. Embracing οἰκοδομή challenges us to be proactive in our encouragement, to offer constructive counsel, and to contribute to a community where everyone can flourish.

Reflection Questions for the Day:

- How can I actively participate in the edification of my church community?

- In what ways can I offer encouragement and support to fellow believers?
- What steps can I take to ensure that my words and actions contribute to building up others in their faith?

Day 48 – κοινωνία (koinōnía) – Fellowship

Greek Word: κοινωνία
English Word: Fellowship
Meaning: A deep, shared communion among believers, characterized by mutual support, love, and unity in Christ.
Bible Reference: Acts 2:42 – "They devoted themselves to the apostles' teaching and the fellowship (κοινωνία) ..."

Devotional Message:

Κοινωνία, or fellowship, is the intimate bond that unites believers as one family in Christ. It goes beyond mere social interaction to encompass a deep, spiritual communion rooted in the love of God and the shared commitment to His teachings. Fellowship provides a safe space where we can encourage one another, share our burdens, and celebrate our victories in faith. It is through this communal life that we experience the true power of God's love, as we become instruments of support and care for one another. In the context of the Church, fellowship is essential for nurturing spiritual growth and fostering a sense of belonging. It calls us to prioritize genuine relationships over superficial connections, ensuring that every member feels valued and heard. Embracing κοινωνία challenges us to invest in our community, building bridges of trust and creating a nurturing environment where God's grace can abound.

Reflection Questions for the Day:

- How do I actively engage in meaningful fellowship within my church community?
- In what ways has genuine fellowship strengthened my faith journey?
- What steps can I take to foster deeper, more authentic relationships with fellow believers?

Day 49 – σῶμα Χριστοῦ (sṓma Christoû) – Body of Christ

Greek Word: σῶμα Χριστοῦ

English Word: Body of Christ

Meaning: The collective community of believers, united in Christ, with each member playing a vital role in the functioning of the whole.

Bible Reference: 1 Corinthians 12:27 – "Now you are the body of Christ, and individually members of it."

Devotional Message:

The concept of σῶμα Χριστοῦ, or the Body of Christ, beautifully illustrates the interconnectedness and interdependence of all believers. Each person within the Body has a unique function, and together we work in harmony to fulfill God's mission on earth. This powerful image reminds us that no member is insignificant, and that every gift and talent is essential for the health and growth of the community. In the Body of Christ, unity and diversity coexist, reflecting the multifaceted nature of God's creative design. Our shared identity as part of this living organism compels us to care for one another, ensuring that every individual is supported and encouraged. This union challenges us to set aside personal ambitions in favor of the collective good, embracing the call to serve and uplift each other. By living as the Body of Christ, we become tangible representations of God's love and grace, shining

His light into every corner of the world.

Reflection Questions for the Day:

- How does understanding myself as part of the Body of Christ impact the way I relate to others?
- In what practical ways can I contribute to the unity and growth of our community?
- How can I use my unique gifts to serve the Church and honor Christ?

Conclusion – The Church

Throughout this week, we have explored the multifaceted nature of the Church as portrayed in the New Testament. We began with ἐκκλησία, understanding that the Church is not a building but a vibrant community of believers united in Christ. The roles of leaders, such as πρεσβύτερος and ἐπίσκοπος, highlight the importance of spiritual maturity, guidance, and accountability in nurturing the community. We then examined the role of διάκονος, emphasizing that serving others is a core aspect of our Christian walk. Through οἰκοδομή and κοινωνία, we learned that edification and fellowship are essential for a healthy and thriving church, where every member contributes to the collective growth. Finally, recognizing ourselves as the σῶμα Χριστοῦ reminds us that we are each integral parts of a greater whole, called to work together in unity and love. Collectively, these truths challenge us to actively participate in the life of the Church, nurturing relationships and embracing our unique roles in God's divine plan. May our commitment to living out these principles deepen our faith and inspire us to be a beacon of hope and unity in the world.

Week 8: Prayer.

Prayer: Communing with God

Prayer is the lifeline of a believer, the sacred connection between us and God. It is more than just asking for things—it is worship, thanksgiving, confession, and intercession. **Philippians 4:6** reminds us, *"Do not be anxious about anything, but in everything by prayer and supplication with thanksgiving let your requests be made known to God."* Through prayer, we express our dependence on Him, align our hearts with His will, and grow in intimacy with our Creator.

Jesus Himself modeled a life of prayer, often withdrawing to seek the Father's presence (Luke 5:16). He taught His disciples how to pray, emphasizing faith, humility, and persistence (Matthew 6:9-13). Prayer is not about eloquence or repetition but about an honest heart that longs to commune with God. It strengthens our spirit, brings peace in trials, and invites God's power into our lives.

As believers, we are called to *"pray without ceasing"* (1 Thessalonians 5:17), making prayer a daily part of our walk with Christ. Whether in joy or sorrow, prayer keeps us rooted in God's presence. Let us approach Him with boldness and faith, knowing He hears, answers, and delights in our prayers.

Day 50 – προσευχή (proseuché) – Prayer

Greek Word: προσευχή
English Word: Prayer
Meaning: A heartfelt conversation with God, involving both praise and petition, through which we draw near to Him.
Bible Reference: Matthew 21:22 – "And whatever you ask in prayer, you will receive, if you have faith."

Devotional Message:

Prayer (προσευχή) is the lifeline of our relationship with God—a sacred dialogue in which we express our deepest hopes, needs, and gratitude. It is not a mere ritual but a dynamic encounter where our hearts meet the heart of God. In prayer, we are invited to cast our cares upon Him, knowing that He listens with compassion and understanding. This conversation with the Divine empowers us, refreshes our spirit, and aligns our will with His. As we learn to pray, we grow in trust and intimacy with God, discovering that even our quietest words are heard by the One who created the universe. Prayer also transforms us; it softens our hearts and prepares us to be more receptive to His guidance. By consistently engaging in προσευχή, we cultivate a habit of reliance on God that sustains us through every season of life.

Reflection Questions for the Day:

- How does my current prayer life reflect a genuine, heartfelt conversation with God?
- In what areas of my life do I need to be more intentional about communicating with the Lord?
- How can I create more quiet moments to practice true prayer throughout my day?

Day 51 – δέησις (déēsis) – Supplication

Greek Word: δέησις
English Word: Supplication
Meaning: An earnest and humble request made to God, expressing our deep needs and dependence on Him.
Bible Reference: Philippians 4:6 – "Do not be anxious about anything, but in everything by prayer and supplication with thanksgiving let your requests be made known to God."

Devotional Message:

Supplication (δέησις) invites us to approach God with a humble and contrite heart, laying our burdens and desires at His feet. It is an act of vulnerability that acknowledges our need for divine intervention in every area of life. When we supplicate, we recognize that no challenge is too big for God and that our limitations can be overcome by His strength. This type of prayer goes beyond routine asking; it is a plea born from deep longing and trust in God's provision. Supplication teaches us to be honest about our struggles, allowing us to release anxieties and fears into His capable hands. Through this process, we experience the comforting presence of a God who cares intimately about every detail of our lives. Embracing δέησις nurtures our faith and reinforces the truth that God is our ever-present help in times of need.

Reflection Questions for the Day:

- In what areas of my life am I hesitant to present my needs to God?
- How does acknowledging my dependence on God through supplication affect my trust in Him?
- What specific burdens do I need to lay before the Lord in prayer today?

Day 52 – ἐντεύξις (enteúksis) – Intercession

Greek Word: ἐντεύξις

English Word: Intercession

Meaning: The act of praying on behalf of others, standing in the gap to seek God's favor and help for them.

Bible Reference: 1 Timothy 2:1 – "I urge, then, first of all, that petitions, prayers, intercession and thanksgiving be made for all people."

Devotional Message:

Intercession (ἐντεύξις) is a selfless form of prayer in which we lift others up before God, asking Him to work in their lives as He does in ours. It is an expression of love and solidarity that demonstrates our care for friends, family, communities, and even those we do not know personally. When we intercede, we enter into the struggles of others, echoing the heart of a compassionate Savior. This prayer calls us to go beyond our personal needs and embrace a wider vision of God's redemptive work. It challenges us to develop empathy and to stand in the gap, trusting that our prayers can bring healing and change. Intercession also deepens our own relationship with God, as we learn to seek His guidance and to understand the power of collective prayer. Embracing ἐντεύξις transforms our hearts into channels of His mercy and grace, fostering unity and hope within the body of Christ.

Reflection Questions for the Day:

- Who in my life or community needs my prayerful intercession today?
- How does interceding for others change my perspective on my own challenges?
- In what ways can I cultivate a regular habit of praying on behalf of those around me?

Day 53 – εὐχαριστία (eucharistía) – Thanksgiving

Greek Word: εὐχαριστία

English Word: Thanksgiving

Meaning: The act of giving grateful praise to God for His blessings, mercy, and faithful provision.

Bible Reference: Colossians 4:2 – "Devote yourselves to prayer, being watchful and thankful."

Devotional Message:

Thanksgiving (εὐχαριστία) is a vital expression of our gratitude to God, acknowledging His continuous goodness in every circumstance. It is more than a polite "thank you"; it is a heartfelt recognition of His countless blessings, even amid trials. When we offer εὐχαριστία, we cultivate an attitude of joy and contentment that transforms our outlook on life. This practice reminds us that every good and perfect gift comes from above and that God's grace is ever-present. Through thanksgiving, our hearts become more receptive to His love, and we develop a deeper trust in His provision. It also serves as a powerful testimony to others, shining a light on the faithfulness of a God who cares. Embracing εὐχαριστία in our daily lives fosters a spirit of humility and joy, helping us to appreciate the richness of God's mercy and kindness.

Reflection Questions for the Day:

- What specific blessings in my life am I grateful for today?
- How can I cultivate a daily practice of thanksgiving, even during difficult times?
- In what ways does expressing gratitude to God influence my overall perspective and mood?

Day 54 – ἀγρυπνία (agrypnía) – Watchfulness

Greek Word: ἀγρυπνία

English Word: Watchfulness

Meaning: A state of alertness and vigilance in prayer, staying spiritually awake and ready for God's guidance.

Bible Reference: Ephesians 6:18 – "And pray in the Spirit on all occasions with all kinds of prayers and requests. With this in mind, be alert and always keep on praying for all the Lord's people."

Devotional Message:

Watchfulness (ἀγρυπνία) calls us to maintain a vigilant and prayerful state of mind, never falling asleep spiritually even when life is busy or challenging. It is an invitation to remain aware of God's presence and to be ready for His guidance at all times. This form of prayer keeps us spiritually attuned, guarding our hearts against complacency and distraction. When we practice ἀγρυπνία, we learn to discern the subtle ways in which God speaks and works around us, ensuring that we are not caught off guard by life's uncertainties. It requires discipline, focus, and a commitment to staying connected with our Creator throughout each day. This vigilance not only fortifies our own faith but also prepares us to support others in their spiritual journeys. Embracing watchfulness transforms our prayer life into a dynamic, ongoing conversation with God that never ceases, no matter the circumstances.

Reflection Questions for the Day:

- How can I remain spiritually alert throughout the day, especially during moments of busyness?
- In what ways does practicing watchfulness in prayer help me discern God's guidance?
- What practical steps can I take to avoid spiritual complacency and maintain a vigilant prayer life?

Day 55 – ἀββᾶ (abba) – Father

Greek Word: ἀββᾶ
English Word: Father

Meaning: An intimate and personal term for God, reflecting the close, childlike relationship we share with Him.

Bible Reference: Mark 14:36 – "And he said, 'Abba, Father, all things are possible for you. Remove this cup from me. Yet not what I will, but what you will.'"

Devotional Message:

The term ἀββᾶ (abba) reveals the intimate, trusting relationship we are invited to have with God as our Father. It expresses a deep sense of closeness and reliance, much like the bond between a loving parent and child. In calling God "Father," we acknowledge His authority and care while also embracing the comfort and security of His unconditional love. This intimate address reminds us that God is not distant or detached but is actively involved in the minutiae of our lives. As we approach Him with the tenderness of a child, we are met with compassion, guidance, and the assurance that we are valued beyond measure. Embracing ἀββᾶ encourages us to lay aside pretenses and connect with God on a profoundly personal level, trusting Him with our deepest fears and highest hopes. This deep connection transforms our prayer life, making it a dynamic, heartfelt conversation that nourishes our soul.

Reflection Questions for the Day:

- How does addressing God as "Father" change my perspective on my relationship with Him?
- In what ways can I cultivate a more intimate, childlike trust in God?
- How does recognizing God's fatherly care influence my responses during times of need?

Day 56 – προσευχομένη (proseuchoménē) – Praying (as

an ongoing act)

Greek Word: προσευχομένη
English Word: Praying (continuous action)
Meaning: The act of engaging in prayer as a sustained, ongoing practice—a lifestyle of communication with God.
Bible Reference: Acts 16:13 – "On the Sabbath we went outside the city gate to the river, where we expected to find a place of prayer. We sat down and spoke to the women who had gathered there."

Devotional Message:

The term προσευχομένη invites us to view prayer not as a one-time event but as an ongoing, integral part of our daily lives. It encourages us to cultivate a lifestyle where prayer is continuous, interwoven into every moment and decision. This ongoing dialogue with God transforms our mundane routines into sacred opportunities for growth and connection. It teaches us to keep our hearts attuned to the presence of God at all times, allowing His guidance to permeate our actions. As we adopt a posture of continual prayer, we experience a deepening of our relationship with the Divine, feeling His presence in both quiet moments and busy hours. This practice nurtures an inner calm and resilience, reminding us that we are never alone in our journey. Embracing προσευχομένη transforms our life into a living prayer, a constant testimony to our reliance on God's grace and wisdom.

Reflection Questions for the Day:

- What practical steps can I take to integrate continual prayer into my daily routine?
- How does viewing prayer as an ongoing practice change my attitude toward challenges?

- In what ways can I remain mindful of God's presence throughout even the busiest parts of my day?

Conclusion – Prayer

Throughout this week, we have journeyed through the diverse and transformative dimensions of prayer. We began with προσευχή, recognizing that genuine prayer is a heartfelt dialogue that brings us closer to God. Our exploration of δέησις revealed the importance of humbly presenting our needs before the Lord, while ἐντεύξις emphasized our call to intercede for others with compassion and faith. The practice of εὐχαριστία reminds us to cultivate a grateful heart, and ἀγρυπνία teaches us to remain vigilant in our spiritual walk. Through addressing God as ἀββᾶ, we experience the intimacy of a loving Father, and by embracing προσευχομένη, we learn to weave prayer continuously into the fabric of our lives. Collectively, these practices form a comprehensive picture of prayer as both an individual and communal discipline that shapes our relationship with God and with one another. May this week's reflections inspire us to pursue a deeper, more vibrant prayer life—one that transforms our hearts, fortifies our faith, and radiates God's love to a world in need.

Week 9: The Word of God.

The Word of God: Living and Powerful

The Word of God is the foundation of our faith, a divine revelation that guides, instructs, and transforms our lives. **Hebrews 4:12** declares, *"For the word of God is living and active, sharper than any two-edged sword, piercing to the division of soul and of spirit, of joints and of marrow, and discerning the thoughts and intentions of the heart."* Unlike any other book, the Bible is inspired by God (2 Timothy 3:16) and carries His authority in every word.

Through Scripture, we come to know God's character, His promises, and His will for our lives. It is a lamp to our feet and a light to our path (Psalm 119:105), providing wisdom, comfort, and correction. The Word sustains us in times of trouble, strengthens our faith, and equips us for every good work.

Jesus Himself, the living Word (John 1:1), used Scripture to resist temptation, teach truth, and reveal God's Kingdom. As His followers, we must not only read but also meditate on and apply His Word daily. Let us hunger for Scripture, allowing it to shape our thoughts, transform our hearts, and lead us in obedience to God's perfect will.

Day 57 – γραφή (graphḗ) – Scripture

Greek Word: γραφή
English Word: Scripture
Meaning: The sacred writings that testify to God's truth and serve as a guide for faith and practice.
Bible Reference: 2 Timothy 3:16 – "All Scripture is breathed out by God and profitable for teaching, for reproof, for correction, and for training in righteousness."

Devotional Message:

Scripture (γραφή) is the foundation upon which our faith is built, a timeless reservoir of God's wisdom and truth. It is through the written Word that God has revealed His character, His promises, and His plan for salvation. Each page of Scripture is not merely historical record but a living message that speaks to us today, guiding our steps and shaping our hearts. Immersing ourselves in the Scriptures invites us to encounter the transformative power of God's truth, enabling us to discern right from wrong and to walk in His light. The Scriptures challenge us to examine our lives and to allow God's corrective grace to refine our character. As we study these sacred texts, we also learn to trust in God's faithfulness, knowing that His promises are sure and His love endures forever. Let every encounter with the Word renew your mind and inspire you to live a life of obedience and praise.

Reflection Questions for the Day:

- How does regular engagement with Scripture influence my daily decisions?
- In what ways can I allow God's Word to shape my thoughts and actions?
- How can I create more opportunities to immerse myself in the truths of Scripture?

Day 58 – ῥῆμα (rhêma) – Word (Spoken)

Greek Word: ῥῆμα

English Word: Word (spoken)

Meaning: A specific utterance or command from God, carrying immediate power and relevance to a particular situation.

Bible Reference: Luke 1:38 – "And Mary said, 'Behold, I am the servant of the Lord; let it be to me according to your word (ῥῆμα).'"

Devotional Message:

The term ῥῆμα highlights the immediacy and personal impact of God's spoken word in our lives. Unlike the written Scriptures, a rhêma often conveys a direct message from God tailored to our circumstances—an encouraging word, a timely command, or a promise of hope. When we hear God's voice through a rhêma, we are reminded that God is not distant; He speaks directly into the fabric of our everyday experiences. This dynamic communication deepens our relationship with Him, making our walk of faith vibrant and responsive. Embracing a rhêma means being attuned to the whispers of the Holy Spirit, ready to receive guidance and to act upon it. It requires a sensitive heart and a willingness to trust God's direction even when it challenges our plans. As you listen for God's spoken word, open your heart to the possibilities of divine inspiration that can transform your life in profound ways.

Reflection Questions for the Day:

- When have I experienced a timely word from God that changed my perspective?
- How can I cultivate a more attentive ear for the Holy Spirit's guidance in my life?
- What steps can I take to ensure that I am receptive to God's spoken word throughout my day?

Day 59 – θεόπνευστος (theópneustos) – God-breathed

Greek Word: θεόπνευστος
English Word: God-breathed
Meaning: Describing the inspiration of Scripture as directly from God, imbued with divine authority and truth.

Bible Reference: 2 Timothy 3:16 – "All Scripture is breathed out by God..."

Devotional Message:

The adjective θεόπνευστος conveys the profound truth that Scripture is not a product of human wisdom alone but is divinely inspired—God-breathed. This means that the words we read in the Bible carry the authority of God Himself, offering us insights that transcend human limitations. Knowing that the Scriptures are the very breath of God brings comfort and assurance, reminding us that His truth is eternal and unchanging. It challenges us to approach the Bible with reverence and humility, recognizing its power to guide, correct, and transform our lives. As we meditate on these inspired words, we are invited to align our thoughts and actions with divine truth. This understanding should ignite within us a passion for deeper study and a commitment to live out the teachings found in God's Word. Embrace the reality that every passage, every verse, is a direct expression of God's love and wisdom for His people.

Reflection Questions for the Day:

- How does knowing that Scripture is "God-breathed" affect the way I read and apply it in my life?
- In what ways can I demonstrate reverence for the inspired Word of God?
- How might I share the transformative nature of God's inspired Word with someone who is seeking truth?

Day 60 – διδασκαλία (didaskalía) – Teaching/Doctrine

Greek Word: διδασκαλία
English Word: Teaching/Doctrine
Meaning: The systematic instruction of the truths of the faith, designed to nurture and guide believers in understanding God's

word.

Bible Reference: 2 Timothy 3:16 – "...profitable for teaching, for reproof, for correction, and for training in righteousness."

Devotional Message:

Didaskalía, or teaching, is central to the nurturing of a mature and vibrant faith. It encompasses not only the impartation of knowledge but also the transformative process by which we learn to live out the truths of the Gospel. Through sound teaching, we are equipped to discern truth from error and to grow in our understanding of God's character and His will for our lives. This systematic instruction builds a solid foundation upon which we can stand firm amid life's uncertainties. As we engage with the doctrines of our faith, our minds are renewed and our hearts are set on a path of righteousness. Teaching challenges us to question, reflect, and ultimately embrace the wisdom that God provides through His Word. It also calls us to share that wisdom with others, making disciples who are well-grounded in the truth of the Gospel. Let every moment of learning draw you closer to the heart of God.

Reflection Questions for the Day:

- What areas of my understanding of Scripture and doctrine need further teaching or clarification?
- How can I actively seek out and apply sound biblical teaching in my daily life?
- In what ways can I share the truths I have learned with others to help strengthen their faith?

Day 61 – μάχαιρα τοῦ πνεύματος (máchaira toû pneumatos) – Sword of the Spirit

Greek Word: μάχαιρα τοῦ πνεύματος

English Word: Sword of the Spirit

Meaning: The Word of God used as a weapon to defend against spiritual attacks and to proclaim truth.

Bible Reference: Ephesians 6:17 – "...and take the helmet of salvation, and the sword of the Spirit, which is the word of God."

Devotional Message:

The phrase μάχαιρα τοῦ πνεύματος illustrates the potent and active role that God's Word plays in our spiritual lives. Just as a sword is a tool of both defense and offense, the Word of God empowers us to confront and overcome the challenges of spiritual warfare. It provides clarity, strength, and authority in moments of doubt and conflict. When we wield the sword of the Spirit, we are reminded that truth is our best defense against the deceptions and temptations of the enemy. This metaphor invites us to not only read and memorize Scripture but to actively apply it in our daily struggles. It encourages us to let the Word penetrate our hearts, transforming us into warriors of light who stand firm in the truth of God. Embracing this powerful tool means that we are continually equipped to discern, resist, and overcome any spiritual attack that comes our way.

Reflection Questions for the Day:

- How can I actively "wield" the sword of the Spirit in my daily life?
- In what situations do I need to rely on God's Word as my defense?
- How might I deepen my understanding of Scripture to better prepare for spiritual challenges?

Day 62 – εὐαγγέλιον (euangélion) – Gospel

Greek Word: εὐαγγέλιον

English Word: Gospel

Meaning: The good news of Jesus Christ's life, death, and resurrection, offering salvation to all who believe.

Bible Reference: Mark 1:1 – "The beginning of the gospel of Jesus Christ..."

Devotional Message:

The Gospel (εὐαγγέλιον) is the heart and hope of the Christian faith—a message of redemption that transforms lives. It proclaims that through Jesus Christ, God has provided a way for humanity to be reconciled to Him and to experience eternal life. This good news is not just a message to be heard; it is a truth to be lived out in every aspect of our lives. Embracing the Gospel means accepting the love, forgiveness, and grace offered by Christ, and then sharing that life-changing message with others. It challenges us to live with a sense of urgency and purpose, knowing that salvation is available to all who believe. The power of the Gospel lies in its ability to break chains, heal wounds, and restore hope in the midst of despair. As you meditate on this truth, allow the good news to renew your spirit and inspire you to be a beacon of hope in a dark world.

Reflection Questions for the Day:

- How has the Gospel transformed my life and perspective?
- In what ways can I share the good news of Jesus Christ with those around me?
- What obstacles do I face in living out the message of the Gospel, and how can I overcome them?

Day 63 – λόγος τῆς ζωῆς (lógos tēs zōḗs) – Word of Life

Greek Word: λόγος τῆς ζωῆς

English Word: Word of Life

Meaning: The message that brings spiritual life and eternal hope, infusing believers with vitality and truth.

Bible Reference: Philippians 2:16 – "…that you may become blameless and innocent, children of God without blemish in the midst of a crooked and twisted generation, among whom you shine as lights in the world."

Devotional Message:

The phrase λόγος τῆς ζωῆς emphasizes that God's Word is not only a set of doctrines but also the source of true life—both in this world and the next. It is the divine message that breathes spiritual vitality into our souls and offers us hope beyond the temporal. This Word of Life transforms our inner being, encouraging us to live with purpose, joy, and unwavering faith. As we embrace this living message, we are reminded that eternal life is not merely a future promise but a present reality manifested in our daily walk with Christ. It calls us to reject the empty pursuits of the world and to focus on the eternal riches found in God's truth. The Word of Life is a light that guides us through darkness, empowering us to live boldly and share His hope with a world in need. Let this message ignite your heart and inspire you to live each day as a testament to the transforming power of God's truth.

Reflection Questions for the Day:

- How does the concept of the "Word of Life" impact my understanding of eternal hope?
- In what ways can I allow God's life-giving Word to transform my daily living?
- How can I actively share the hope found in the Word of Life with those who are searching for meaning?

Conclusion – The Word of God

Throughout this week, we have explored the diverse dimensions of the Word of God, witnessing how it shapes, defends, and transforms our lives. We began with γραφή, recognizing Scripture as the timeless testimony of God's truth and the foundation of our faith. We then discovered the immediacy of a ῥῆμα—a specific, spoken word that speaks directly into our circumstances. The concept of θεόπνευστος reassured us that the Bible is divinely inspired, carrying the very breath of God. Through διδασκαλία, we saw how teaching nurtures our understanding and empowers us to live out God's truth. The metaphor of the μάχαιρα τοῦ πνεύματος revealed the active role of God's Word in spiritual warfare, while the εὐαγγέλιον reminds us of the transformative good news of salvation. Finally, the λόγος τῆς ζωῆς encapsulates the life-giving, eternal hope that the Word brings to every believer. Collectively, these insights form a powerful mosaic of truth that not only fortifies our faith but also challenges us to become active carriers of God's living Word. May our hearts be continually renewed by His truth, and may we share its transformative power with a world in desperate need of life.

Week 10: Worship.

Worship: A Heart Devoted to God

Worship is more than a song or a Sunday service—it is a lifestyle of surrender, devotion, and love for God. **John 4:24** says, *"God is spirit, and those who worship Him must worship in spirit and truth."* True worship flows from a heart that honors God not just with words, but with obedience and reverence. It is our response to His greatness, reflecting our gratitude, adoration, and love.

Worship is not confined to a church building; it happens in our everyday lives—through prayer, obedience, service, and even in how we treat others. It is recognizing God's worthiness and offering ourselves fully to Him (Romans 12:1). Whether through singing praises, meditating on His Word, or serving in humility, worship connects us to the heart of God.

Jesus set the ultimate example of worship through His life of complete submission to the Father's will. As His followers, we are called to worship Him with all that we are—our time, talents, and hearts. Let our worship be genuine and passionate, exalting God in every aspect of our lives. When we live as true worshipers, we reflect His glory and draw closer to His presence.

Day 64 – προσκυνέω (proskynéō) – Worship

Greek Word: προσκυνέω
English Word: Worship
Meaning: To bow down or show reverence to God, offering Him honor and adoration.
Bible Reference: John 4:24 – "God is spirit, and those who worship him must worship in spirit and truth."

Devotional Message:

Worship (προσκυνέω) is the heart's expression of reverence for God, a deliberate act of honoring Him above all else. It calls us to humble ourselves before the Creator, recognizing His majesty and sovereignty in every aspect of our lives. True worship is not confined to a building or a specific ritual; it is a lifestyle where our thoughts, words, and deeds reflect our deep adoration for the Lord. When we worship, we acknowledge that God alone is worthy of our praise and that our lives are meant to be a living sacrifice. This act of worship connects us to the divine, inviting the Holy Spirit to work in us and through us. As we surrender our hearts in worship, we experience transformation and renewal, enabling us to face life's challenges with hope and confidence. Embracing προσκυνέω means allowing every moment to be an opportunity to exalt God in spirit and truth.

Reflection Questions for the Day:

- In what ways can I make worship a continuous expression of my heart both in public and in private?
- How does acknowledging God's supremacy transform my daily attitude and decisions?
- What practical steps can I take today to express sincere worship in all that I do?

Day 65 – λατρεία (latreía) – Service/Worship

Greek Word: λατρεία

English Word: Service or Worship

Meaning: The devoted service or acts of worship rendered to God, reflecting a life of dedication and sacrificial love.

Bible Reference: Romans 12:1 – "I appeal to you therefore, brothers, by the mercies of God, to present your bodies as a living sacrifice, holy and acceptable to God, which is your spiritual worship (λατρεία)."

Devotional Message:

Latreía encompasses the idea that true worship is not only what we say but also how we serve. It calls us to offer our whole selves— body, mind, and spirit—as a living sacrifice to God. This service is a tangible expression of our gratitude and love for Him and is characterized by acts of kindness, integrity, and generosity. Through λατρεία, our everyday actions become an extension of our worship, turning ordinary moments into holy encounters with the Divine. It challenges us to examine our motives, ensuring that our service is done with humility and selflessness, echoing the heart of Christ. When we engage in this form of worship, we build a bridge between our personal devotion and the needs of others, making our faith visible in the world. Embracing λατρεία means recognizing that every act of service is an opportunity to glorify God and to invite others into the beauty of His kingdom.

Reflection Questions for the Day:

- How do my daily actions reflect a lifestyle of devoted service to God?
- In what ways can I transform mundane tasks into acts of worship?
- What opportunities do I have today to serve others as an expression of my love for God?

Day 66 – ὕμνος (hýmnos) – Hymn

Greek Word: ὕμνος

English Word: Hymn

Meaning: A song of praise that exalts God's character and recounts His mighty works, used in both private and corporate worship.

Bible Reference: Ephesians 5:19 – "Addressing one another in psalms and hymns and spiritual songs, singing and making melody to the Lord with your heart."

Devotional Message:

A hymn (ὕμνος) is a powerful vehicle of worship, lifting our hearts in melody to celebrate the greatness of God. Through singing, we recall His wondrous deeds and proclaim His unfailing love, transforming our emotions and uniting us as a community of believers. Hymns serve as a reminder of the timeless truths of Scripture, engraving God's promises and faithfulness in our hearts. When we sing, we not only express joy and gratitude but also find solace in His presence during trials. The act of singing worship nurtures our souls and helps us to internalize the message of the Gospel. It invites us to participate in a tradition that has sustained generations of believers, linking us to the heritage of faith. Embracing ὕμνος means allowing the beauty of music to penetrate our spirit, enabling us to worship God in both word and melody.

Reflection Questions for the Day:

- How does singing hymns enhance my personal worship experience?
- In what ways can I use music to draw closer to God and remember His promises?
- How can I incorporate more intentional moments of musical worship into my daily routine?

Day 67 – δοξάζω (doxázō) – Glorify

Greek Word: δοξάζω
English Word: Glorify
Meaning: To honor, praise, and exalt God by acknowledging His

supreme greatness and works.

Bible Reference: John 17:1 – "Father, the hour has come; glorify your Son that the Son may glorify you."

Devotional Message:

To doxázō is to lift God up in every aspect of our lives, proclaiming His majesty and reflecting His light in a dark world. Glorifying God means that we intentionally direct our praise not only through words but also through our actions, attitudes, and interactions. It is an act of worship that acknowledges God's sovereignty, His loving kindness, and His creative power. When we seek to glorify God, we put aside personal ambitions and allow His glory to shine through us, transforming even our struggles into testimonies of His grace. This call to glorification invites us to examine every sphere of our lives—our work, our relationships, and our community—to ensure that they reflect the goodness of our Creator. In doing so, we become living testimonies to the wonder of God's love and power. Embracing δοξάζω challenges us to make it our highest goal to honor God in every thought and deed.

Reflection Questions for the Day:

- What are practical ways I can glorify God in my daily life?
- How does focusing on God's glory change my priorities and decisions?
- In what situations can I choose to set aside my own ambitions to honor God instead?

Day 68 – σέβομαι (sébomai) – Reverence

Greek Word: σέβομαι
English Word: Reverence
Meaning: A deep respect and awe for God that manifests in our attitude, speech, and actions, acknowledging His holiness and

majesty.

Bible Reference: Acts 17:17 – "So he reasoned in the synagogue with both Jews and God-fearing Greeks, as well as in the marketplace day by day, with those who happened to be there."

Devotional Message:

Reverence (σέβομαι) is the heartfelt recognition of God's supreme holiness, prompting us to approach Him with deep respect and awe. This attitude of honor shapes our entire demeanor, influencing the way we speak, act, and interact with others. When we live in reverence of God, we are continually aware of His presence and the majesty of His works, which in turn inspires humility and obedience. This profound respect is not based on fear alone but on a deep appreciation of His loving character and mighty power. It transforms our approach to worship, turning every act into a meaningful encounter with the Divine. As we cultivate a lifestyle of reverence, we learn to value the sacred in every aspect of our lives, from the quiet moments of prayer to the bustling energy of our daily routines. Embracing σέβομαι invites us to live with an ongoing awareness of God's grandeur, allowing that awareness to direct all our thoughts and actions.

Reflection Questions for the Day:

- In what ways can I cultivate a deeper sense of reverence for God in my daily life?
- How does living with a spirit of awe impact my interactions and decisions?
- What changes can I make to ensure that every aspect of my life reflects my respect for God's holiness?

Day 69 – εὐλογέω (eulogéō) – Bless

Greek Word: εὐλογέω

English Word: Bless

Meaning: To speak well of or to confer favor upon someone, invoking God's goodness and grace upon them.

Bible Reference: Ephesians 1:3 – "Blessed be the God and Father of our Lord Jesus Christ, who has blessed us in Christ with every spiritual blessing in the heavenly places."

Devotional Message:

To eulogéō is to actively pronounce God's favor and goodness upon others, reflecting a heart filled with gratitude and love. Blessing is a powerful expression of worship, as it acknowledges that all we have comes from God's gracious hand. When we bless others, we become channels of His mercy, sharing the hope and joy that flow from our relationship with Him. This act of blessing encourages unity and builds up the body of Christ, as we remind one another of God's abundant grace. It transforms our relationships, turning our interactions into opportunities for grace and encouragement. As we make it a habit to bless those around us, we participate in God's redemptive work, spreading His light into every corner of our communities. Embracing εὐλογέω not only honors God but also cultivates a spirit of generosity and love in our own hearts.

Reflection Questions for the Day:

- How can I intentionally speak blessings over those in my life today?
- In what ways does blessing others reflect my gratitude for God's gifts?
- How might my words and actions become instruments of God's favor and goodness in my community?

Day 70 – λειτουργία (leitourgía) – Liturgy/Ministry

Greek Word: λειτουργία
English Word: Liturgy or Ministry
Meaning: The structured service of God, encompassing the public acts of worship and the organized ministry that edifies the Church.
Bible Reference: Philippians 2:17 – "Even if I am to be poured out as a drink offering upon the sacrificial service (λειτουργία) of your faith, I am glad and rejoice with you all."

Devotional Message:

Leitourgía embodies the concept of serving God through organized, intentional acts of worship and ministry. It is the framework through which believers come together to offer collective praise, to learn from one another, and to carry out God's mission in the world. This form of worship is both a privilege and a responsibility, as it calls us to use our gifts for the edification of the Church and the glory of God. When we participate in liturgy, we are reminded that our individual acts of worship blend into a greater symphony of praise that honors God's sovereignty and grace. It challenges us to serve selflessly and to view our time in community as an essential element of our spiritual growth. Through λειτουργία, the church becomes a vibrant, living organism that reflects the unity and diversity of God's people. Embracing this structured service not only deepens our personal worship but also strengthens the bonds of fellowship among believers.

Reflection Questions for the Day:

- In what ways does participating in structured worship or ministry enrich my relationship with God?
- How can I contribute my unique gifts to the liturgical life of my church community?

- What can I learn from my involvement in ministry that can further deepen my personal faith?

Conclusion – Worship

Throughout this week, we have journeyed through the many facets of worship, discovering that it is far more than a momentary act—it is a lifestyle. We began with προσκυνέω, learning that true worship arises from a heart that humbly exalts God in spirit and truth. We then saw that λατρεία transforms everyday actions into acts of service that honor God. Through ὕμνος, our souls are lifted in song, while δοξάζω challenges us to actively proclaim God's majesty. The practice of σέβομαι instills in us a deep reverence that shapes all our interactions, and εὐλογέω reminds us of the power of blessing as an expression of gratitude. Finally, λειτουργία illustrates the beauty of communal worship and organized ministry that unites believers in a shared purpose. Together, these truths reveal that worship is an all-encompassing expression of our love for God—one that engages our hearts, minds, and bodies every day. May these insights inspire us to live lives marked by continual praise, heartfelt service, and a deep commitment to glorifying our Creator in every aspect of our journey.

Week 11: Sin and Repentance.

Sin and Repentance: Turning Back to God

Sin is the great barrier that separates humanity from God. It is not just wrongdoing—it is rebellion against His holiness and a turning away from His perfect will. **Romans 3:23** reminds us, *"For all have sinned and fall short of the glory of God."* Sin leads to spiritual death, but God, in His mercy, offers us a way back through repentance.

Repentance is more than feeling sorry for our sins; it is a heartfelt decision to turn away from sin and return to God. **Acts 3:19** urges us, *"Repent therefore, and turn back, that your sins may be blotted out."* True repentance involves confession, a change of heart, and a commitment to live according to God's ways. It is not about perfection, but about surrender—acknowledging our need for Christ and allowing His grace to transform us.

God's love is always ready to receive a repentant heart. No sin is too great for His forgiveness, and no one is beyond His redemption. When we repent, we find restoration, freedom, and new life in Christ. Let us daily examine our hearts, turn away from sin, and walk in the joy of God's forgiveness and grace.

Day 71 – ἁμαρτία (hamartía) – Sin

Greek Word: ἁμαρτία
English Word: Sin
Meaning: The state of missing the mark; a moral failing that separates us from God's perfect standard.
Bible Reference: Romans 3:23 – "For all have sinned and fall short of the glory of God."

Devotional Message:

Sin (ἁμαρτία) is the fundamental condition that disrupts our relationship with God, representing the ways in which we fall short of His holy standard. It is not merely an action but a condition of the heart—a deviation from God's truth that affects every aspect of our lives. Understanding sin helps us recognize our need for God's mercy and the grace available through Christ's sacrifice. As we confront our own sinfulness, we are invited to humble ourselves before God, acknowledging our imperfections and our deep need for forgiveness. This honest recognition is the first step in the healing process, drawing us toward repentance and restoration. Sin can create feelings of guilt and separation, but it also opens the door for the redemptive work of Christ. By facing sin with honesty, we learn to depend on God's grace and move toward a life that honors Him.

Reflection Questions for the Day:

- In what areas of my life do I see the mark of sin most clearly?
- How does acknowledging my sin deepen my reliance on God's grace?
- What steps can I take today to confront and confess the ways I have fallen short?

Day 72 – παράπτωμα (paráptōma) – Trespass

Greek Word: παράπτωμα
English Word: Trespass
Meaning: A specific offense or transgression against God's law, often reflecting a violation of trust.
Bible Reference: Ephesians 2:1 – "And you were dead in the trespasses and sins…"

Devotional Message:

Trespass (παράπτωμα) refers to a deliberate or negligent act that violates God's law—a personal crossing of boundaries that disrupts our communion with Him. It carries the connotation of stepping aside from the correct path and harming the trust God has placed in us. When we commit a trespass, we not only disobey God but also damage our relationships with others. This awareness should lead us to a deep sense of regret, prompting us to seek reconciliation with God and those we have wronged. Recognizing our trespasses is essential for a genuine process of repentance, as it brings our faults into the light. In acknowledging these transgressions, we open ourselves to the transformative power of confession and forgiveness. Ultimately, addressing our trespasses is part of our journey back to spiritual wholeness and the restoration of God's favor.

Reflection Questions for the Day:

- What trespasses have I committed that need to be brought before God?
- How has my understanding of trespass helped me see the importance of personal accountability?
- In what ways can I actively seek to restore trust and mend broken relationships?

Day 73 – ἀνομία (anomía) – Lawlessness

Greek Word: ἀνομία

English Word: Lawlessness

Meaning: A state of disregard for God's law, characterized by a rebellious or unruly nature.

Bible Reference: 1 John 3:4 – "Everyone who makes a practice of sinning also practices lawlessness; sin is lawlessness."

Devotional Message:

Lawlessness (ἀνομία) goes beyond isolated acts of disobedience to describe a condition of the heart that rejects the order and goodness of God's law. It reflects a deep-seated rebellion that disrupts the natural order God designed for our lives. This state of lawlessness is dangerous because it leads us further away from the truth and breaks the harmony intended for humanity. Recognizing lawlessness within ourselves is a call to serious self-examination and to the realization that our way of living is fundamentally at odds with God's will. It challenges us to repent and to seek the discipline and guidance of God's Word. Confronting our own lawlessness allows the Holy Spirit to work in us, transforming chaos into order and disobedience into obedience. Ultimately, overcoming lawlessness is key to restoring our relationship with God and living in the freedom of His righteous rule.

Reflection Questions for the Day:

- In what ways have I exhibited lawlessness by neglecting God's standards?
- How can I cultivate a heart that values God's law above my own desires?
- What practical steps can I take to replace rebellious behavior with obedience to God?

Day 74 – ἐξομολόγησις (exomológēsis) – Confession

Greek Word: ἐξομολόγησις

English Word: Confession

Meaning: The act of admitting and declaring one's sins before God, acknowledging wrongdoing and seeking His forgiveness.

Bible Reference: James 5:16 – "Therefore, confess your sins to one another and pray for one another, that you may be healed."

Devotional Message:

Confession (ἐξομολόγησις) is a crucial step in our journey toward healing and reconciliation with God. It involves the humble acknowledgment of our sins and the willingness to face our shortcomings openly. By confessing our sins, we break the power of secrecy and shame, allowing God's grace to work freely in our lives. This act is not meant to condemn us, but to bring us into a state of restoration and renewal. Confession fosters accountability, builds community, and strengthens our resolve to pursue righteousness. It is a moment of vulnerability that leads to deeper intimacy with God, as we experience His boundless mercy and forgiveness. Embracing confession reminds us that no sin is too great to be forgiven when we come before a loving and compassionate God.

Reflection Questions for the Day:

- What sins or shortcomings do I need to confess to God today?
- How has confessing my sins previously led to a deeper experience of God's forgiveness?
- In what ways can I create an environment of openness and accountability in my relationships?

Day 75 – μεταμέλεια (metaméleia) – Regret/Remorse

Greek Word: μεταμέλεια
English Word: Regret/Remorse
Meaning: A deep, sincere sorrow for one's sins and a genuine desire to change one's behavior.
Bible Reference: Matthew 27:3 – "When he saw that he had failed,

Peter returned to the chief priests and the elders, and said, 'I am guilty of having betrayed the innocent.'" *(Note: This verse illustrates the heart of remorse, though it does not use the Greek word explicitly.)*

Devotional Message:

Regret or remorse (μεταμέλεια) is the emotional response that follows the recognition of our sins—a heartfelt sorrow that leads us to repentance. It goes beyond mere regret over consequences; it is a deep mourning for the ways in which our actions have grieved our loving God. This sincere remorse is the catalyst that compels us to turn away from sin and to seek restoration. It is an essential part of the repentance process, as it demonstrates that we value our relationship with God more than the fleeting pleasures of disobedience. In experiencing μεταμέλεια, our hearts are softened, and we become more receptive to God's healing and transformative power. It encourages us to make a committed change, aligning our lives with the truth of God's Word. Embracing true remorse allows us to leave behind the guilt of the past and to move forward into the light of God's forgiveness.

Reflection Questions for the Day:

- What areas of my life stir deep remorse, prompting me to seek change?
- How does genuine regret over my sins motivate me to pursue a more righteous path?
- In what ways can I nurture a heart that is quick to repent and open to God's healing?

Day 76 – ἐπιστρέφω (epistréphō) – Turn Back

Greek Word: ἐπιστρέφω

English Word: Turn Back

Meaning: To return or repent—making a deliberate change in direction, away from sin and toward God.

Bible Reference: Acts 3:19 – "Repent therefore, and turn back, that your sins may be blotted out."

Devotional Message:

To turn back (ἐπιστρέφω) is to make a decisive commitment to leave behind a life of sin and to return to the loving embrace of God. This act of repentance is both a spiritual and practical turning point, marking the moment when we choose to follow God's ways instead of our own. It requires courage and humility, as we acknowledge that our previous paths have led us away from truth and life. By turning back, we invite God to restore us, heal our brokenness, and set us on a new course defined by His love and righteousness. This turning is not a one-time event but a continuous process, as we daily choose to follow the guidance of the Holy Spirit. It transforms our identity, replacing the old self with a renewed spirit dedicated to living for God. Embracing ἐπιστρέφω renews our hope and reaffirms our commitment to walk in the light of His truth.

Reflection Questions for the Day:

- What areas of my life require a decisive turning back from sin?
- How can I cultivate a daily attitude of returning to God when I stray?
- In what practical ways can I demonstrate my commitment to change and renewal?

Day 77 – κατάνυξις (katányxis) – Piercing (of Heart)/Conviction

Greek Word: κατάνυξις
English Word: Piercing (of Heart)/Conviction
Meaning: A deep, penetrating awareness of sin that leads to genuine sorrow and the desire to reform.
Bible Reference: Acts 2:37 – "Now when they heard this, they were cut to the heart (κατάνυξις)..."

Devotional Message:

Κατάνυξις describes the powerful conviction that seizes our heart when we truly recognize the weight of our sin. It is a piercing awareness that leaves us with a profound sense of sorrow for the ways we have strayed from God's truth. This conviction is not meant to condemn us but to awaken us to the need for repentance and transformation. When our hearts are pierced by the realization of our sin, we are moved to action—seeking God's forgiveness and committing to a change of life. Such deep conviction fosters humility, drawing us closer to God and opening our hearts to His restorative grace. It is a painful yet necessary experience that propels us on the journey toward spiritual renewal. Embracing κατάνυξις means accepting that God's love can use our brokenness to create a more refined, obedient, and loving heart.

Reflection Questions for the Day:

- When have I experienced a deep conviction that led me to change my ways?
- How can I remain sensitive to the prompting of the Holy Spirit when I fall short?
- What practical steps can I take to allow this conviction to transform my actions and attitudes?

Conclusion – Sin and Repentance

Throughout this week, we have confronted the stark realities of sin and the redemptive process of repentance. We began by recognizing ἁμαρτία, the universal condition of sin that separates us from the holiness of God. We then examined παράπτωμα, a trespass that breaches the boundaries of His law, and ἀνομία, a state of lawlessness that disrupts the divine order. As we moved into ἐξομολόγησις, we learned the power of confession to bring hidden sins into the light, paving the way for healing. The heartfelt μεταμέλεια we experienced opened our eyes to the sorrow that leads to transformation, while ἐπιστρέφω encouraged us to actively turn away from sin and toward God. Finally, through κατάνυξις, we encountered the piercing conviction that motivates lasting change. Together, these truths underscore the need for continuous repentance, drawing us ever closer to the mercy and grace of our Savior. May the lessons of this week inspire us to live lives marked by humility, accountability, and a deep commitment to walking in the light of God's forgiveness.

Week 12: Forgiveness.

Forgiveness: The Heart of God's Love

Forgiveness is at the core of the Gospel—it is God's gift of grace to a sinful world. **Ephesians 1:7** declares, *"In Him we have redemption through His blood, the forgiveness of our trespasses, according to the riches of His grace."* Through Christ's sacrifice on the cross, we are fully pardoned, set free from the penalty of sin, and restored to a right relationship with God. His forgiveness is not based on our worthiness but on His boundless mercy.

Just as we have been forgiven, we are called to extend forgiveness to others. Jesus taught in **Matthew 6:14**, *"For if you forgive others their trespasses, your heavenly Father will also forgive you."* Forgiving others is not always easy, but it is essential for our spiritual health and peace. Holding onto bitterness only enslaves us, while forgiveness releases us to experience true freedom.

Forgiveness does not excuse wrongdoing, but it reflects God's love by choosing mercy over revenge. When we forgive, we mirror Christ's grace and allow healing to take place in our hearts. May we live as people of grace, extending the same forgiveness we have received, and walking in the joy of God's mercy.

Day 78 – ἄφεσις (áphesis) – Forgiveness

Greek Word: ἄφεσις
English Word: Forgiveness
Meaning: The act of releasing someone from the guilt or punishment of sin; a divine pardon that restores relationship with God.
Bible Reference: Luke 24:47 – "and that repentance and

forgiveness of sins should be proclaimed in his name to all nations."

Devotional Message:

Forgiveness (ἄφεσις) is at the heart of the Gospel, revealing God's profound mercy toward a fallen world. When God forgives, He releases us from the burden of our past transgressions, offering a fresh start in His grace. This divine pardon is not earned but freely given through the sacrifice of Jesus Christ, who bore the penalty for our sins. Experiencing ἄφεσις transforms our hearts by replacing guilt with hope and despair with joy. It is through forgiveness that we are reconciled to God and invited to live in freedom and love. As we receive this gift, we are also called to extend forgiveness to others, mirroring the mercy we have received. Embracing ἄφεσις means accepting that no sin is too great to be washed away by God's love, and it empowers us to walk in newness of life.

Reflection Questions for the Day:

- In what ways have I experienced God's forgiveness in my life?
- How does knowing I am forgiven change the way I view my past mistakes?
- What steps can I take today to extend forgiveness to someone who has hurt me?

Day 79 – χαρίζομαι (charízomai) – To Graciously Forgive

Greek Word: χαρίζομαι
English Word: To Graciously Forgive
Meaning: To freely extend pardon and mercy to others, mirroring God's generous forgiveness toward us.
Bible Reference: Ephesians 4:32 – "Be kind to one another, tenderhearted, forgiving one another, as God in Christ forgave

you."

Devotional Message:

The verb χαρίζομαι challenges us to forgive others in the same gracious manner that God forgave us. This act of forgiving freely goes beyond merely overlooking offenses—it is an intentional, loving response that breaks the cycle of bitterness. When we choose to χαρίζομαι, we release the burden of anger and invite healing into our relationships. Gracious forgiveness softens our hearts, enabling us to see the humanity and vulnerability in others. It transforms conflicts into opportunities for reconciliation and growth, reflecting the radical love of Christ. Practicing this forgiveness also liberates us from holding onto past hurts, allowing us to experience peace and renewed hope. By forgiving as we have been forgiven, we become living testimonies of God's grace and mercy.

Reflection Questions for the Day:

- How can I practice gracious forgiveness in a situation where I feel hurt?
- What steps can I take to let go of past grievances and extend mercy to others?
- How does forgiving others help me experience the freedom of God's grace in my own life?

Day 80 – ἱλαστήριον (hilastḗrion) – Mercy Seat/Atonement

Greek Word: ἱλαστήριον
English Word: Mercy Seat/Atonement
Meaning: The place or means by which atonement is made, symbolizing the sacrificial offering that reconciles us with God.

Bible Reference: Romans 3:25 – "whom God put forward as a propitiation by his blood, to be received by faith."

Devotional Message:

The term ἱλαστήριον refers to the profound mystery of atonement—God's way of covering our sins and restoring our relationship with Him. It calls to mind the sacrificial offering of Christ, whose blood was shed to satisfy divine justice and bring about forgiveness. This imagery reminds us that our reconciliation with God was achieved at a tremendous cost, highlighting the depth of His love. The mercy seat is not only a symbol of forgiveness but also a source of hope, assuring us that no sin is beyond the reach of God's redeeming grace. As we reflect on ἱλαστήριον, we are invited to approach God with gratitude, recognizing that His atoning sacrifice has made us whole. This truth should move us to live lives that honor His gift of salvation and to extend compassion to others. Embracing the atonement means living in the freedom that comes from being cleansed by the blood of Christ.

Reflection Questions for the Day:

- How does the concept of atonement through the mercy seat deepen my appreciation for Christ's sacrifice?
- In what ways can I live a life that reflects the freedom of being made whole through His atoning work?
- How can I share the hope of God's redeeming love with someone who feels burdened by guilt?

Day 81 – λογίζομαι (logízomai) – Not to Count (Sins) Against

Greek Word: λογίζομαι
English Word: To Reckon/Count (Not to Count Sins Against)

Meaning: To deliberately choose not to hold one's sins or transgressions against them, extending forgiveness as God does.

Bible Reference: 2 Corinthians 5:19 – "that is, in Christ God was reconciling the world to himself, not counting their trespasses against them."

Devotional Message:

The act of λογίζομαι in the context of forgiveness is a powerful reminder that God does not hold our sins against us once we come to Him in repentance. This concept calls us to release the burden of past offenses, choosing instead to embrace the grace that has been freely given. When God refrains from counting our sins, He offers us a fresh start—a new identity in Christ. This freedom encourages us to live with confidence and gratitude, knowing that our mistakes no longer define us. Moreover, as we receive this mercy, we are called to extend the same grace to others by not holding their faults against them. Practicing λογίζομαι transforms our relationships and fosters an environment of unconditional love and acceptance. In doing so, we reflect the heart of God, who reconciles and restores us through His unfailing love.

Reflection Questions for the Day:

- What past sins or mistakes do I need to let go of so that they no longer burden my relationship with God?
- How can I mirror God's grace by choosing not to count others' faults against them?
- In what ways does living free from the weight of past sins change my daily interactions and outlook?

Day 82 – ἀποκατάστασις (apokatástasis) – Restoration

Greek Word: ἀποκατάστασις

English Word: Restoration
Meaning: The act of being restored to a former state of wholeness, especially in one's relationship with God.
Bible Reference: Acts 3:21 – "heaven must receive him until the time comes for God to restore everything, as he promised long ago through his holy prophets."

Devotional Message:

Restoration (ἀποκατάστασις) is the beautiful promise that God can renew and rebuild our lives after we have experienced the pain of sin. It signifies not only the forgiveness of our transgressions but also the healing of our hearts and the mending of relationships that have been broken. In God's timing, restoration brings us back to a place of spiritual wholeness and purpose, affirming that no failure or mistake is beyond repair. This process calls us to trust in His plan, even when the path to renewal seems uncertain. As we allow God to restore us, we are transformed from the inside out, equipped to live in alignment with His perfect will. The promise of ἀποκατάστασις offers hope and a future filled with possibility—a future where past wounds give way to divine healing. Embracing restoration means stepping into the fullness of life that God intends for us, marked by renewal, joy, and unwavering hope.

Reflection Questions for the Day:

- What areas of my life need restoration and renewal through God's grace?
- How can I trust God more deeply as He works to restore what has been broken in my heart?
- In what ways can I actively participate in the process of spiritual restoration in my relationships?

Day 83 – καθαρισμός (katharismós) – Cleansing

Greek Word: καθαρισμός

English Word: Cleansing

Meaning: The process of being purified from sin and defilement, restored to spiritual purity by God's grace.

Bible Reference: 1 John 1:7 – "but if we walk in the light, as he is in the light, we have fellowship with one another, and the blood of Jesus his Son cleanses us from all sin."

Devotional Message:

Cleansing (καθαρισμός) is the divine act of purifying our hearts and lives from the stains of sin. Through the blood of Jesus, we are made clean, not by our efforts but by God's unmerited mercy. This spiritual cleansing is a continuous process that renews our minds and transforms our actions. It invites us to live in the light of truth, free from the burdens of guilt and shame. As we allow God to cleanse us, we become vessels of His love, ready to reflect His holiness in our interactions. This purification is both a comfort and a call to live righteously, knowing that our past does not define our future. Embracing καθαρισμός means accepting God's invitation to daily renewal, where every moment is an opportunity to step closer to His perfect will.

Reflection Questions for the Day:

- How has God's cleansing power changed my life and freed me from guilt?
- In what ways can I maintain a lifestyle that reflects ongoing spiritual purity?
- What practical steps can I take to ensure that I remain receptive to God's cleansing work in my heart?

Day 84 – ἐλεήμων (eleḗmōn) – Merciful

Greek Word: ἐλεήμων

English Word: Merciful

Meaning: Showing compassion, kindness, and forgiveness, reflecting the character of God's love toward all.

Bible Reference: Luke 6:36 – "Be merciful, even as your Father is merciful."

Devotional Message:

Being merciful (ἐλεήμων) is a defining characteristic of God's nature—a compassionate response that extends forgiveness and kindness even when it is undeserved. This mercy flows from a deep understanding of our own need for forgiveness and calls us to extend that same grace to others. It transforms our hearts, softening any hardness that may have taken root through past hurts or disappointments. Embracing a merciful spirit means looking beyond the faults of others to see the inherent value and potential for change in every person. It challenges us to act with empathy, offering a hand of support and a word of encouragement instead of judgment. As we reflect on God's mercy toward us, we are empowered to replicate that love, building bridges where there were walls and healing relationships that had been broken. Living mercifully invites us to become true reflections of our Father's heart, spreading compassion in a world that desperately needs it.

Reflection Questions for the Day:

- In what ways can I extend mercy to those who have wronged me or hurt me?
- How does remembering God's mercy toward me shape my interactions with others?
- What practical steps can I take to cultivate a more compassionate and forgiving heart?

Conclusion – Forgiveness

Throughout this week, we have journeyed deep into the transformative power of forgiveness. We began by exploring ἄφεσις, the divine release from guilt that restores our relationship with God, and learned to extend that same grace through χαρίζομαι. We then contemplated the mystery of ἱλαστήριον, the mercy seat that symbolizes Christ's atoning sacrifice, and embraced the liberating practice of λογίζομαι—choosing not to hold our sins or the sins of others against us. As we moved forward, ἀποκατάστασις reminded us of God's promise to restore and renew our lives, while καθαρισμός illustrated the continual purification available to us through His blood. Finally, ἐλεήμων called us to mirror God's merciful nature in every interaction, demonstrating compassion as our Father has shown to us. Together, these truths form a comprehensive picture of forgiveness—a process that heals, renews, and transforms us. May the lessons of this week inspire us to live in the freedom of God's grace, continually extending forgiveness to ourselves and to others, and to walk in the light of His redeeming love.

Reflection Questions for the Week:

- How has this week's focus on forgiveness transformed my understanding of God's grace?
- What areas of my life need the healing and renewal that forgiveness offers?
- How can I actively extend the forgiveness I have received to those around me, and what steps will I take to make that a daily practice?

Week 13: Grace and Mercy.

Grace and Mercy: God's Undeserved Love

Grace and mercy are two of the greatest gifts God extends to us. Though we are sinners, God's grace gives us what we do not deserve—salvation, eternal life, and His boundless love. At the same time, His mercy spares us from the punishment we do deserve. **Ephesians 2:8-9** declares, *"For by grace you have been saved through faith, and this is not your own doing; it is the gift of God, not a result of works, so that no one may boast."*

God's mercy is seen in His patience and compassion toward us. Instead of condemning us, He provides a way to be restored through Jesus Christ. His grace is freely given—not because of our works, but because of His great love. As recipients of this grace and mercy, we are called to extend the same to others, forgiving as we have been forgiven and loving as we have been loved.

Living in God's grace means walking in freedom, knowing that we are no longer defined by our past but by His love. His mercy renews us daily, reminding us that His kindness leads us to repentance. Let us embrace His grace and extend His mercy, reflecting His heart to the world.

Day 85 – χάρις (cháris) – Grace

Greek Word: χάρις
English Word: Grace
Meaning: The unmerited favor and kindness of God that saves, sustains, and transforms us despite our unworthiness.
Bible Reference: Ephesians 2:8 – "For by grace you have been saved through faith. And this is not your own doing; it is the gift of God."

Devotional Message:

Grace (χάρις) is the heart of the Gospel, revealing that salvation is not earned but freely given by a loving God. It is the divine favor that covers our shortcomings and empowers us to live a transformed life. When we embrace grace, we understand that our past does not determine our future, for God's love reaches beyond every fault. This unmerited gift encourages us to stand in awe of God's generosity and to trust Him completely. Grace not only saves us but continually renews us, providing strength for every trial and hope in every moment. As we receive grace, we are called to extend it to others, forgiving and loving without measure. Embracing χάρις transforms our hearts, freeing us to live boldly and compassionately in the light of God's mercy.

Reflection Questions for the Day:

- How does understanding God's grace change my perspective on my past mistakes?
- In what ways can I extend the same grace I've received to those around me?
- What steps can I take today to deepen my trust in God's unmerited favor?

Day 86 – Ἔλεος (éleos) – Mercy

Greek Word: ἔλεος

English Word: Mercy

Meaning: Compassionate kindness that relents judgment, offering forgiveness and relief to the undeserving.

Bible Reference: Luke 6:36 – "Be merciful, even as your Father is merciful."

Devotional Message:

Mercy (ἔλεος) is the tender compassion that God shows us despite our failings, inviting us into a relationship marked by forgiveness and hope. It is through His mercy that we experience relief from guilt and find the courage to start anew. When we reflect on God's mercy, we are moved to act with similar kindness toward others, softening hearts hardened by pride or pain. Mercy calls us to look beyond retribution and to embrace the healing power of forgiveness. It is a reminder that every act of compassion echoes God's loving response to our shortcomings. As we receive His mercy, we learn to let go of bitterness and extend a hand of help to those in need. Embracing ἔλεος transforms our lives, nurturing an environment of grace and reconciliation in our relationships.

Reflection Questions for the Day:

- How have I experienced God's mercy in times of need?
- In what specific ways can I practice mercy toward someone who has wronged me?
- How does showing mercy reflect the character of my Heavenly Father?

Day 87 – οἰκτιρμός (oiktirmós) – Compassion

Greek Word: οἰκτιρμός

English Word: Compassion

Meaning: Deep empathy and tenderness that compels us to alleviate the suffering of others.

Bible Reference: Colossians 3:12 – "Put on then, as God's chosen ones, holy and beloved, compassionate hearts…"

Devotional Message:

Compassion (οἰκτιρμός) calls us to see the world through God's eyes—to feel the pain of others as our own and to act with loving kindness. It goes beyond mere sympathy; it is an active, heartfelt response that leads us to serve and uplift those in distress. When we cultivate compassion, our hearts are softened, enabling us to reach out to the hurting with empathy and practical help. This genuine care is a reflection of Christ's own tender heart toward the downtrodden and oppressed. Compassion motivates us to break down barriers, extend forgiveness, and build bridges of understanding. As we grow in οἰκτιρμός, we become instruments of God's healing love, spreading hope where there is despair. Embracing compassion transforms our interactions, making our community a testament to the love and care of our Savior.

Reflection Questions for the Day:

- Who in my life or community is in need of compassionate care today?
- How can I cultivate a deeper sense of empathy for others' struggles?
- What practical steps can I take to demonstrate Christ-like compassion in my daily actions?

Day 88 – μακροθυμέω (makrothyméō) – Long-suffering/Patient

Greek Word: μακροθυμέω
English Word: To be patient/Long-suffering
Meaning: The endurance of hardship with a calm spirit, exhibiting perseverance and understanding over time.
Bible Reference: 2 Peter 3:9 – "The Lord is not slow to fulfill his promise as some count slowness, but is patient toward you..."

Devotional Message:

Long-suffering (μακροθυμέω) is the patient endurance that reflects God's own forbearance with us, even when we falter or cause pain. It is a virtue that calls us to bear with one another's weaknesses and to allow time for healing and growth. In a fast-paced world, practicing patience teaches us to trust in God's perfect timing and to find peace amid delays. This enduring quality strengthens our relationships, enabling us to extend grace in the face of frustration and misunderstanding. When we exercise μακροθυμέω, we emulate the patient love of Christ, who continuously forgives and renews. It challenges us to be steadfast in our commitment to love, even when the journey is long and arduous. Embracing long-suffering transforms our hearts, empowering us to live with a resilient spirit that remains hopeful and compassionate under pressure.

Reflection Questions for the Day:

- In what situations do I need to exercise more patience and endurance?
- How does understanding God's patience toward me help me extend it to others?
- What practices can I adopt to cultivate a spirit of long-suffering in my daily life?

Day 89 – δωρεά (dōreá) – Gift

Greek Word: δωρεά
English Word: Gift
Meaning: A gracious offering given freely by God, reflecting His unmerited favor and blessing.
Bible Reference: John 4:10 – "Jesus answered her, 'If you knew the gift (δωρεά) of God, and who it is that is saying to you, "Give me a drink," you would have asked him, and he would have given you living water.'"

Devotional Message:

The concept of δωρεά reminds us that every blessing we experience is a gift from God—unearned and lavishly bestowed upon us. It underscores that our salvation, our strength, and even our daily provisions come not from our own works but from the generous heart of our Creator. Recognizing this gift fills us with gratitude and a sense of humility, as we realize that we are recipients of divine kindness. As we receive the gift of God's love, we are inspired to share that same generosity with others, creating a ripple effect of kindness and hope. This understanding challenges us to live with an open heart, always ready to give and to receive graciously. The gift of δωρεά transforms our perspective on life, encouraging us to see every moment as an opportunity to celebrate God's goodness. Embracing this gift fuels a spirit of thankfulness that sustains us through every season of life.

Reflection Questions for the Day:

- How does knowing that every blessing is a gift from God change my attitude toward life's challenges?
- In what ways can I actively share the gifts I have received with those around me?
- How can I cultivate a heart of gratitude that continually acknowledges God's gracious provision?

Day 90 – πλουτέω ἐν ἐλέει (ploutéō en eléei) – Rich in Mercy

Greek Word: πλουτέω ἐν ἐλέει
English Word: Rich in Mercy
Meaning: Overflowing with compassion and kindness, reflecting the abundant mercy that God bestows upon His people.

Bible Reference: Ephesians 2:4 – "But because of his great love for us, God, who is rich in mercy…"

Devotional Message:

To be rich in mercy (πλουτέω ἐν ἐλέει) is to experience and exhibit the abundant compassion of God in every aspect of our lives. It signifies that His mercy is not measured in scarcity but overflows, touching every area of our brokenness. When we recognize that God is rich in mercy, we are encouraged to respond with a generous heart toward others, forgiving and comforting without reserve. This richness challenges us to abandon a spirit of retribution and instead embrace a lifestyle marked by kindness and understanding. It transforms our relationships by creating space for healing and reconciliation, as we extend to others the mercy we have received. Living in this reality reminds us that no matter how often we fall, God's mercy is ever-present to restore and renew us. Embracing a rich mercy compels us to be conduits of God's grace, shining His light into the darkest corners of our world.

Reflection Questions for the Day:

- How does understanding God's abundant mercy inspire me to treat others with compassion?
- In what ways can I cultivate a lifestyle that reflects richness in mercy?
- What steps can I take to forgive more freely and extend kindness to those who hurt me?

Day 91 – Θρόνος τῆς χάριτος (thrónos tēs cháritos) – Throne of Grace

Greek Word: θρόνος τῆς χάριτος

English Word: Throne of Grace

Meaning: The divine seat from which God dispenses unmerited favor, mercy, and help to those who approach Him in faith.

Bible Reference: Hebrews 4:16 – "Let us then with confidence draw near to the throne of grace, that we may receive mercy and find grace to help in time of need."

Devotional Message:

The phrase θρόνος τῆς χάριτος encapsulates the invitation to approach God's very presence with boldness and humility. It reminds us that God's grace is not hidden or distant but is accessible to all who seek Him. From this throne, we receive mercy, comfort, and strength to navigate life's challenges. It is a place of divine encounter where our deepest needs are met with the overflowing generosity of our Heavenly Father. Approaching the throne of grace transforms our perspective on struggle, as we are reassured that we are never alone in our battles. This sacred invitation calls us to abandon fear and approach God with confidence, knowing that His favor abounds in every moment of need. Embracing this truth empowers us to live with hope, assured that His grace will sustain and uplift us through all circumstances.

Reflection Questions for the Day:

- How does drawing near to God's throne of grace transform my approach to life's challenges?
- In what ways can I cultivate the confidence to seek mercy and help in my daily struggles?
- How does the promise of the throne of grace influence my relationship with God and others?

Conclusion – Grace and Mercy

Throughout this week, we have journeyed through the rich landscape of God's grace and mercy, exploring how these divine attributes transform our lives. We began by understanding χάρις, the unmerited favor that saves and sustains us, and learned to extend that same grace through the act of χαρίζομαι. We then contemplated the mystery of atonement at the ἱλαστήριον, where Christ's sacrifice makes reconciliation possible, and embraced the freedom of letting go through λογίζομαι. Our hearts were softened by the promise of restoration (ἀποκατάστασις) and purified through the continual work of καθαρισμός. We then experienced ἐλεήμων, the call to mirror God's own merciful nature, which challenges us to live with compassion and forgiveness. Each day, from the understanding of grace to the rich mercy of our Heavenly Father, has deepened our appreciation for the transformative power of God's love. May these truths inspire us to continually live in the freedom of grace and extend mercy to others, becoming beacons of hope and healing in a world longing for divine compassion.

Reflection Questions for the Week:

- How has this week deepened my understanding of grace and mercy in my personal walk with God?
- What areas of my life most need the healing power of God's forgiveness and restoration?
- In what specific ways can I reflect the grace and mercy I have received onto those around me?
- How does living in the light of God's rich mercy change my daily decisions and relationships?
- What practical steps can I take to ensure that I remain open to God's continual cleansing and renewal?
- How can I use my experiences of grace and mercy to encourage others who struggle with guilt and despair?

- What commitments will I make this week to actively embody the love and compassion of my Heavenly Father?

Week 14: Faith and Trust.

Faith and Trust: Anchored in God's Promises

Faith and trust are the foundation of our relationship with God. **Hebrews 11:1** defines faith as, *"the assurance of things hoped for, the conviction of things not seen."* It is believing in God's promises even when circumstances seem uncertain. Trust, on the other hand, is our unwavering confidence in His character, knowing that He is faithful and His plans are good.

Life is filled with challenges that test our faith, but God calls us to walk by faith, not by sight (2 Corinthians 5:7). Trusting Him means surrendering our fears, doubts, and control, knowing that He holds our future in His hands. When we put our faith in Him, we experience peace that surpasses understanding, even in the midst of trials.

Abraham trusted God when called to step into the unknown; Peter walked on water when his eyes were fixed on Jesus. Likewise, our faith grows as we rely on God daily, choosing to trust Him even when we don't see the full picture. Let us hold fast to His promises, knowing that He is always faithful. When we place our trust in Him, we will never be shaken, for He is our firm foundation.

Day 92 – πιστεύω (pisteúō) – To Believe

Greek Word: πιστεύω
English Word: To Believe
Meaning: To trust or have faith in God and His promises, relying on His truth for life and salvation.
Bible Reference: John 3:16 – "For God so loved the world that he gave his only Son, that whoever believes in him should not perish but have eternal life."

Devotional Message:

Believing (πιστεύω) is the very foundation of our relationship with God. It means placing our trust wholeheartedly in the One who has promised us eternal life and unwavering love. When we believe, we surrender our doubts and allow God's truth to shape our understanding of the world. This act of faith is not passive—it requires active commitment, even when circumstances seem uncertain. Trusting in God means accepting that His plan is greater than our own and that His timing is perfect. As we grow in belief, our hearts are transformed by the power of His grace, and our lives begin to reflect the hope of the Gospel. Embracing πιστεύω invites us into a deeper intimacy with God, as we rest in the assurance that He is always faithful.

Reflection Questions for the Day:

- How does my belief in God shape my daily decisions and attitudes?
- In what areas of my life do I struggle to trust God fully, and why?
- How can I strengthen my commitment to living by faith, even in uncertainty?

Day 93 – πειθώ (peithṓ) – To Persuade/Be Confident

Greek Word: πειθώ
English Word: To Persuade/Be Confident
Meaning: To be convinced and confident in God's truth, resulting in a bold declaration of our faith.
Bible Reference: Galatians 5:10 – "For all who rely on works are under a curse; for it is written, 'Cursed is everyone who does not abide by all things written in the Book of the Law, and do them.'"
(While this verse challenges self-reliance, it reminds us that our

confidence must be rooted in God's Word.)

Devotional Message:

The verb πειθώ calls us to a confidence that is not shaken by the opinions of others or by our own limitations. It is a conviction that comes from a deep understanding of God's promises and a personal encounter with His faithfulness. When we are persuaded by His truth, we become bold witnesses for Christ, confidently sharing the hope that has been placed in our hearts. This certainty challenges us to leave behind the uncertainties of the world and to stand firm in the assurance that God's Word is our firm foundation. Embracing πειθώ means that our trust is not based on human logic alone but on the divine power and wisdom of our Creator. As we grow in this confidence, our lives become a testimony to the transformative power of faith, inspiring others to seek the same assurance in God. Let us allow His truth to persuade our hearts and embolden our spirit.

Reflection Questions for the Day:

- What specific promises of God bolster my confidence in Him?
- How can I actively demonstrate a bold trust in His Word in my everyday life?
- In what ways can I encourage others to stand firm in their faith through my own example?

Day 94 – πεποίθησις (pepoíthēsis) – Confidence

Greek Word: πεποίθησις
English Word: Confidence
Meaning: A firm, unwavering trust and assurance in God's reliability and truth.
Bible Reference: 2 Corinthians 3:4 – "Such is the confidence that

we have through Christ toward God."

Devotional Message:

Confidence (πεποίθησις) in the Lord means knowing deep in our hearts that God is true and reliable. This kind of trust goes beyond intellectual assent—it permeates our entire being and empowers us to face life's challenges with courage. When we have πεποίθησις, our faith becomes a shield against doubt, enabling us to stand strong even in the midst of trials. This assurance is built upon our personal experiences of God's faithfulness and His constant presence in our lives. It is a confidence that grows as we meditate on His promises and see them fulfilled in our own journeys. Embracing this certainty inspires us to step out in faith, confident that no obstacle is too great when God is our guide. Let our lives be a reflection of the unwavering confidence we have in our Savior, encouraging others to find hope in His steadfast love.

Reflection Questions for the Day:

- What past experiences have strengthened my confidence in God's faithfulness?
- How does a deep sense of confidence in the Lord affect my response to life's challenges?
- In what ways can I share this assurance with others who struggle with doubt?

Day 95 – ὑπόστασις (hypóstasis) – Assurance

Greek Word: ὑπόστασις

English Word: Assurance

Meaning: The underlying reality and substance of our faith—a steadfast confidence in the promises of God.

Bible Reference: Hebrews 11:1 – "Now faith is the assurance (ὑπόστασις) of things hoped for, the conviction of things not seen."

Devotional Message:

Assurance (ὑπόστασις) is the very substance of our faith—it is the deep-rooted confidence that what we hope for is real and that God's promises will come to pass. This unwavering certainty is not based on what we can see, but on the spiritual conviction that God is at work in our lives. It empowers us to move forward with hope even when circumstances appear bleak, knowing that our faith is anchored in eternal truths. When we experience true assurance, our hearts are filled with peace and resilience, enabling us to endure trials with a steadfast spirit. It is a gift of the Holy Spirit that assures us of God's continual presence and unfailing love.

Embracing ὑπόστασις means living with a certainty that transcends the temporal, allowing us to trust in God's eternal plan. May this assurance encourage us to walk boldly in faith, secure in the knowledge of His promises.

Reflection Questions for the Day:

- What does assurance in God's promises look like in my daily life?
- How can I nurture a deeper sense of certainty in my faith during times of uncertainty?
- In what ways does the conviction of things not seen empower me to persevere?

Day 96 – ἀσφαλής (asphalḗs) – Sure/Secure

Greek Word: ἀσφαλής

English Word: Sure/Secure

Meaning: Completely reliable and unshaken by doubt; having a secure foundation in God.

Bible Reference: Acts 22:30 – "For I am convinced that neither death nor life, neither angels nor rulers, neither things present nor things to come..." *(This verse underscores the certainty and security found in our faith.)*

Devotional Message:

To be ἀσφαλής means to experience a security in our relationship with God that is unyielding, even amid life's storms. When we find ourselves secure in God's love and promises, no external circumstance can shake our inner peace. This sense of safety comes from knowing that our foundation is built upon the unchanging truth of His Word. In a world filled with uncertainty, our secure standing in Christ enables us to navigate challenges with confidence and hope. Embracing ἀσφαλής transforms our perspective, as we trust that nothing—no matter how daunting—can undermine the steadfast promises of God. This security encourages us to step out boldly, knowing that our lives are anchored in eternal truths. Let us rest in the assurance that, through Christ, we are safe, secure, and unshakeable.

Reflection Questions for the Day:

- What areas of my life need a stronger sense of security in God's promises?
- How does feeling secure in Christ influence my decision-making and outlook on life?
- What steps can I take to deepen my understanding of God's unchanging nature?

Day 97 – βεβαιόω (bebaióō) – To Confirm/Establish

Greek Word: βεβαιόω

English Word: To Confirm/Establish
Meaning: To make firm, to set with certainty; to confirm the truth of God's promises in our lives.
Bible Reference: 1 Corinthians 1:8 – "He will also confirm you to the end, so that you may be blameless on the day of our Lord Jesus Christ."

Devotional Message:

The act of βεβαιόω involves affirming the truths of our faith and establishing our lives on the solid foundation of God's Word. It is the process by which our trust in Him is strengthened and made resilient against doubt. When God confirms His promises, our hearts are fortified, and our faith becomes unshakeable. This divine confirmation encourages us to live boldly, knowing that every promise of God is sure and will come to fruition. It inspires us to actively seek His guidance, trusting that He will establish our steps and secure our future. Embracing βεβαιόω means that we are not left to our own devices; instead, we rest in the certainty that God's purpose will prevail. Let this assurance empower us to witness His faithfulness in every facet of our lives.

Reflection Questions for the Day:

- How has God confirmed His promises in my life, and how do I recognize His faithfulness?
- In what ways can I actively establish my trust in God amidst uncertainties?
- How can I help others see the evidence of God's reliable promises through my testimony?

Day 98 – θαρσέω (tharséō) – Take Courage

Greek Word: θαρσέω
English Word: Take Courage

Meaning: To be bold and confident; to act with bravery in the face of challenges, trusting in God's strength.

Bible Reference: Matthew 9:2 – "And behold, some people brought to him a paralytic, lying on a bed. And when Jesus saw their faith, he said to the paralytic, 'Take heart, my son; your sins are forgiven.'"

Devotional Message:

Taking courage (θαρσέω) means stepping forward with boldness, knowing that God's strength is made perfect in our weakness. It is a call to act in faith even when the path ahead seems daunting. When we embrace this courage, we recognize that the challenges we face are opportunities for God's power to be revealed in our lives. This boldness is not born of self-reliance but of the assurance that God is with us every step of the way. As we take heart, we move beyond our fears and limitations, trusting that His guidance will lead us to victory. The courage to act in faith transforms our perspective, allowing us to see obstacles not as insurmountable barriers, but as stepping stones toward greater trust and maturity. Embracing θαρσέω invites us to live with a spirit of audacity, confident in the promise that our God is ever-present and ever-powerful.

Reflection Questions for the Day:

- In what areas of my life do I need to take greater courage and step out in faith?
- How does remembering God's past faithfulness empower me to face current challenges?
- What specific actions can I take today to demonstrate bold trust in God?

Conclusion – Faith and Trust

Throughout this week, we have journeyed through the core elements of faith and trust, discovering that a life anchored in God is one marked by unwavering confidence. We began by embracing πιστεύω, the simple yet profound act of believing in God's promises—a trust that forms the foundation of our spiritual lives. As we moved into πειθώ, we learned to be convinced and bold in our testimony, a reflection of the deep confidence that comes from knowing His truth. Our exploration of πεποίθησις and ὑπόστασις deepened our understanding of what it means to have firm assurance in the unseen and eternal. We then discovered the comfort of being ἀσφαλής in God's unchanging nature, which secures our hearts against life's uncertainties. Through βεβαιόω, we saw how God confirms His promises in our lives, establishing our faith as unshakeable. Finally, θαρσέω challenged us to take courageous steps, trusting in His strength to overcome every obstacle. Collectively, these truths remind us that faith is not a fleeting feeling but a dynamic, daily commitment to trust in the One who is always faithful. May our lives be a testament to this steadfast trust, inspiring us and others to live boldly in the light of God's eternal promises.

Reflection Questions for the Week:

- How have the themes of belief, assurance, and courage transformed my understanding of faith?
- In what ways can I better incorporate a daily practice of trusting God in both small and significant decisions?
- What steps can I take to be an encouraging witness of God's faithfulness to those around me?
- How does embracing my identity as secure in Christ change my response to challenges?
- In what areas do I still struggle with doubt, and how can I address them through prayer and Scripture?

- How can I actively share the confidence I have in God's promises with others facing uncertainty?
- What commitments will I make this week to continue growing in faith and trust in our loving Savior?

Week 15: Spiritual Warfare.

Spiritual Warfare: Standing Firm in Christ

Spiritual warfare is the unseen battle between good and evil, where believers are called to stand firm against the schemes of the enemy. **Ephesians 6:12** reminds us, *"For we do not wrestle against flesh and blood, but against the rulers, against the authorities, against the cosmic powers over this present darkness, against the spiritual forces of evil in the heavenly places."* The enemy seeks to weaken our faith, fill us with fear, and distract us from God's purpose, but through Christ, we have victory.

God has equipped us with spiritual armor—the belt of truth, the breastplate of righteousness, the shield of faith, the helmet of salvation, and the sword of the Spirit, which is the Word of God (Ephesians 6:13-17). Through prayer, faith, and reliance on Scripture, we can resist the enemy's attacks.

We do not fight this battle alone. Christ has already overcome the world (John 16:33), and His power is greater than any force of darkness. When we stand firm in Him, no weapon formed against us shall prosper (Isaiah 54:17). Let us remain vigilant, clothed in God's armor, and confident that victory belongs to those who stand in His strength.

Day 99 – πανοπλία (panoplía) – Full Armor

Greek Word: πανοπλία
English Word: Full Armor
Meaning: The complete set of spiritual defenses God provides for believers to stand against the attacks of the enemy.
Bible Reference: Ephesians 6:11 – "Put on the whole armor of God, that you may be able to stand against the schemes of the devil."

Devotional Message:

The concept of πανοπλία, or full armor, reminds us that our battle is not fought with physical weapons but with spiritual resources supplied by God. Every piece of this armor—the belt of truth, the breastplate of righteousness, the shield of faith, the helmet of salvation, and the sword of the Spirit—is designed to protect and empower us. When we intentionally "put on" this armor, we acknowledge our dependence on God and His provision to face spiritual challenges. This armor enables us to stand firm in the face of temptation, discouragement, and the subtle deceptions of the enemy. It serves as a constant reminder that our strength comes from God alone and that we are not left to our own devices in the midst of conflict. As we daily equip ourselves with His armor, our faith is fortified, and our spiritual resilience grows. Embracing πανοπλία transforms our perspective on warfare, shifting our focus from our own weaknesses to God's all-sufficient power.

Reflection Questions for the Day:

- How am I intentionally "putting on" the full armor of God each day?
- In what areas of my life do I feel vulnerable, and how can God's armor provide protection?
- How does remembering God's provision empower me to face spiritual challenges?

Day 100 – πάλη (pálē) – Struggle/Wrestle

Greek Word: πάλη
English Word: Struggle/Wrestle
Meaning: The ongoing battle against spiritual forces, requiring perseverance and active engagement in faith.
Bible Reference: Ephesians 6:12 – "For we do not wrestle against flesh and blood, but against the rulers, against the authorities,

against the cosmic powers over this present darkness, against the spiritual forces of evil in the heavenly places."

Devotional Message:

The word πάλη captures the essence of our spiritual struggle, emphasizing that our battle is not against people but against unseen spiritual forces. It reminds us that the challenges we face require perseverance, prayer, and reliance on God's strength. Every moment of wrestling with spiritual adversity is an opportunity to grow in faith and to develop character that reflects Christ's resilience. As we engage in this struggle, we are not defeated but are being refined and prepared for greater victories. The struggle itself becomes a testimony to God's transforming power when we persist despite our limitations. In the midst of conflict, we learn to lean on God's promises and to trust that His strength is made perfect in our weakness. Embracing πάλη calls us to be active participants in our spiritual growth, fighting not out of fear but out of a bold confidence in the victory that is already ours in Christ.

Reflection Questions for the Day:

- What spiritual struggles am I currently facing, and how can I view them as opportunities for growth?
- How can I rely more on God's strength in my moments of weakness?
- In what ways can I transform my perspective on conflict into a journey of perseverance and trust in God?

Day 101 – μεθοδεία (methodeía) – Schemes/Stratagems

Greek Word: μεθοδεία
English Word: Schemes/Stratagems
Meaning: The cunning tactics or deceptive plans employed by the

enemy to undermine our faith and disrupt God's work.

Bible Reference: Ephesians 6:11 – "...stand against the schemes (μεθοδεία) of the devil."

Devotional Message:

The term μεθοδεία highlights the reality that our adversary employs crafty and deceptive strategies to lure us away from God's truth. Recognizing these schemes is the first step in resisting temptation and spiritual deception. As believers, we must be vigilant, discerning the subtle plots that seek to weaken our resolve and compromise our testimony. By understanding the nature of these stratagems, we are better prepared to counter them with the truth of God's Word and the power of the Holy Spirit. This awareness not only protects us but also empowers us to stand firm in our identity as children of God. When we expose and reject these schemes, we affirm our commitment to live in obedience and integrity. Embracing μεθοδεία in our study of Scripture helps us to identify and dismantle the enemy's tactics, ensuring that we remain steadfast in our spiritual journey.

Reflection Questions for the Day:

- What are some common schemes I have noticed in my spiritual walk that try to distract or discourage me?
- How can I better equip myself to recognize and resist deceptive tactics?
- In what ways does grounding myself in God's truth empower me to dismantle the enemy's strategies?

Day 102 – βέλος (bélos) – Arrow/Dart

Greek Word: βέλος
English Word: Arrow/Dart
Meaning: A projectile used by the enemy to strike at our

vulnerabilities—representing temptations or attacks designed to harm our spirit.

Bible Reference: Ephesians 6:16 – "In all circumstances take up the shield of faith, with which you can extinguish all the flaming arrows (βέλος) of the evil one."

Devotional Message:

The imagery of βέλος evokes the picture of small yet piercing attacks that the enemy launches to weaken our resolve. Each arrow represents a specific temptation, doubt, or discouragement aimed at our hearts. The beauty of God's design is that He provides us with the shield of faith to deflect these assaults. When we actively wield our shield, we are able to extinguish these flaming darts before they can wound us deeply. This practice of guarding our hearts with faith requires diligence, prayer, and a constant remembrance of God's promises. It is a call to be alert and discerning, so that we do not fall prey to every attack. Embracing the reality of βέλος helps us to understand that while the enemy's arrows are numerous, God's provision for our defense is greater.

Reflection Questions for the Day:

- What "arrows" or temptations do I frequently encounter, and how can I guard my heart against them?
- How can I more effectively use the shield of faith in my daily life?
- What steps can I take to be more alert to the subtle attacks that aim to undermine my spiritual strength?

Day 103 – Θυρεός (thyreós) – Shield

Greek Word: Θυρεός
English Word: Shield
Meaning: The protective barrier provided by God's power and our

faith, designed to deflect the enemy's attacks.

Bible Reference: Ephesians 6:16 – "...take up the shield of faith, with which you can extinguish all the flaming arrows of the evil one."

Devotional Message:

The shield (θυρεός) is an essential piece of our spiritual armor, symbolizing the defense that faith provides against the forces of evil. It is by this shield that we are able to block the harmful arrows of doubt, fear, and temptation. This protective barrier is not something we generate on our own; it is the result of trusting in God's promises and embracing His truth. When we hold fast to our faith, we create a spiritual defense that repels the enemy's attacks and preserves our inner peace. The shield of faith also empowers us to stand firm, even in the face of overwhelming adversity. It serves as a reminder that our security lies not in our strength but in the unchanging nature of God's love. Embracing θυρεός means actively cultivating a robust faith that continuously defends and sustains us through life's battles.

Reflection Questions for the Day:

- How do I actively nurture the shield of faith in my daily life?
- In what situations have I experienced the protective power of God's faith?
- How can I strengthen my spiritual defenses against the enemy's attacks?

Day 104 – περικεφαλαία (perikephalaía) – Helmet

Greek Word: περικεφαλαία
English Word: Helmet
Meaning: The protective covering of our mind provided by salvation, safeguarding our thoughts from the enemy's deceptions.

Bible Reference: Ephesians 6:17 – "...and the helmet of salvation."

Devotional Message:

The helmet (περικεφαλαία) represents the mind's protection that comes from our salvation in Christ. Just as a helmet shields our head from injury, the assurance of salvation guards our thoughts and renews our understanding. It is a constant reminder that we are redeemed and that our identity is secured in Christ. This spiritual protection enables us to reject the lies and discouragements that the enemy tries to implant in our minds. With the helmet of salvation, we are equipped to think clearly and to discern truth from deception. It empowers us to stand firm in the knowledge that our eternal security is guaranteed by God's grace. Embracing περικεφαλαία calls us to guard our minds by meditating on Scripture and living in the light of our redeemed identity.

Reflection Questions for the Day:

- What steps can I take to protect my mind with the assurance of salvation?
- How does the knowledge of my identity in Christ help me combat negative or deceptive thoughts?
- In what ways can I regularly renew my mind through God's Word to strengthen my spiritual helmet?

Day 105 – ῥύομαι (rhýomai) – To Rescue/Deliver

Greek Word: ῥύομαι

English Word: To Rescue/Deliver

Meaning: The act of being saved or delivered from danger, particularly from the snares of the enemy through God's intervention.

Bible Reference: 2 Timothy 4:18 – "The Lord will rescue (ῥύομαι) me from every evil deed and bring me safely into his heavenly kingdom."

Devotional Message:

To ῥύομαι means to be rescued from peril—a promise that God is actively involved in delivering us from every trap set by the enemy. This assurance is a testament to His protective power and loving care, reminding us that no matter how dire our circumstances may seem, God is our ultimate deliverer. When we face spiritual battles, we can be confident that He will intervene and provide a way out. The act of rescue is both a moment of divine intervention and an ongoing promise that we are never abandoned. It calls us to trust in God's timing and to lean on His strength in moments of weakness. Embracing ῥύομαι encourages us to live with a spirit of hope and gratitude, knowing that our future is secure in His hands. May this promise of rescue inspire us to remain faithful and courageous in our daily walk.

Reflection Questions for the Day:

- How have I experienced God's rescuing power in my life?
- In what situations do I need to lean more fully on God for deliverance?
- How can I cultivate a deeper trust in His promise to rescue me from every danger?

Conclusion – Spiritual Warfare

Throughout this week, we have explored the spiritual arsenal that God provides to equip us for battle against the forces of darkness. We began by examining πανοπλία, the full armor of God, which reminds us to be continuously prepared for the enemy's schemes. We then delved into the nature of our struggle (πάλη), learning that our battle is not against flesh and blood but against spiritual forces. As we uncovered the cunning tactics (μεθοδεία) of the enemy, we also learned how to defend ourselves against his piercing attacks (βέλος) by wielding the shield of faith (θυρεός). The helmet of salvation (περικεφαλαία) protects our mind and identity, while the promise of rescue (ῥύομαι) assures us that God is always present to deliver us from danger. Collectively, these truths remind us that spiritual warfare is not fought in isolation but with the full power and provision of God. May the insights from this week embolden us to stand firm, to rely on God's strength, and to walk victoriously in His power, knowing that the battle is already won through Christ.

Reflection Questions for the Week:

- How has understanding the components of spiritual warfare equipped me to face daily challenges?
- In what ways can I more consistently "put on" the full armor of God in my life?
- What specific spiritual disciplines can I adopt to remain vigilant against the enemy's schemes?
- How can I share the hope and assurance of God's protection with fellow believers?
- In what situations have I experienced God's deliverance, and how does that strengthen my faith?
- What steps can I take to guard my mind and spirit through prayer and Scripture?
- How does acknowledging the spiritual battle inspire me to live boldly and courageously for Christ?

Week 16: Eschatology (End Times).

Eschatology: Hope in the End Times

Eschatology, the study of the end times, is not meant to create fear but to strengthen our hope in Christ's return. **Matthew 24:36** reminds us, *"But concerning that day and hour no one knows, not even the angels of heaven, nor the Son, but the Father only."* While we do not know the exact time, Scripture assures us that Jesus will come again to establish His eternal Kingdom.

The Bible speaks of signs of the end—wars, natural disasters, moral decline, and increasing deception (Matthew 24:6-14). Yet, believers are called to remain steadfast, watching and preparing, not in fear but in faith. The return of Christ is a promise that justice will prevail, sin will be defeated, and God's people will dwell with Him forever.

As we await His coming, we are called to live with urgency, sharing the Gospel and walking in holiness. The end times remind us that this world is temporary, and our true citizenship is in heaven (Philippians 3:20). Let us stay faithful, trusting in God's perfect plan, knowing that for those who belong to Christ, the end is not destruction but the beginning of eternal glory with our Savior.

Day 106 – ἀποκάλυψις (apokálypsis) – Revelation

Greek Word: ἀποκάλυψις
English Word: Revelation
Meaning: The unveiling or disclosure of divine mysteries and the ultimate destiny of the world, as revealed by God.
Bible Reference: Revelation 1:1 – "The revelation of Jesus Christ, which God gave him to show to his servants the things that must soon take place."

Devotional Message:

Revelation (ἀποκάλυψις) invites us to peer beyond the present and catch a glimpse of God's unfolding plan for history. This divine unveiling is not meant to induce fear, but to encourage believers with the promise of God's ultimate victory over evil. As we study Revelation, we encounter symbols and prophecies that call us to live with eternal perspective, recognizing that the present world is temporary. The message of Revelation urges us to remain faithful and vigilant, knowing that the culmination of all things is under God's sovereign control. It challenges us to discern the spiritual realities behind the visions and to trust that God's truth will prevail even when mystery surrounds the end times. In embracing ἀποκάλυψις, we are reminded to hold fast to hope and to find comfort in the assurance that God's plan is perfect and purposeful. Let this prophetic word guide you to live with anticipation and readiness for the fulfillment of His promises.

Reflection Questions for the Day:

- How does understanding Revelation impact my view of current events and future hope?
- In what ways can I live with an eternal perspective amidst daily challenges?
- How can I find encouragement in the promise that God's ultimate plan will prevail?

Day 107 – παρουσία (parousía) – Coming/Presence

Greek Word: παρουσία
English Word: Coming/Presence
Meaning: The anticipated arrival or presence of Christ at the end of the age, signifying His return in glory.
Bible Reference: 1 Thessalonians 4:15 – "For this we declare to you

by a word from the Lord, that we who are alive, who are left until the coming (παρουσία) of the Lord, will not precede those who have fallen asleep."

Devotional Message:

The term παρουσία encapsulates the hopeful expectation of Christ's return, a moment when His presence will be unmistakably revealed to all. This promise of His coming is a source of great comfort and urgency, urging believers to remain watchful and prepared. The anticipation of Christ's arrival reminds us that history is moving toward a divinely ordained climax where every injustice will be set right. In our daily walk, the hope of His presence encourages us to live righteously and to spread the Gospel with passion. The promise of παρουσία is a call to live in readiness, maintaining spiritual vigilance and perseverance. It fuels our hope in the midst of trials and assures us that our struggles are temporary compared to the eternal glory that awaits. Embracing this promise helps us to prioritize our relationship with Christ as we await His triumphant return.

Reflection Questions for the Day:

- How does the promise of Christ's coming influence my priorities and daily living?
- In what practical ways can I remain spiritually vigilant as I wait for His return?
- How can I share the hope of His imminent presence with those who are discouraged?

Day 108 – Ἀρμαγεδδών (Armageddõn) – Armageddon

Greek Word: Ἀρμαγεδδών
English Word: Armageddon

Meaning: The prophesied site of the final, cataclysmic battle between the forces of good and evil at the end of the age.

Bible Reference: Revelation 16:16 – "And they assembled them at the place that in Hebrew is called Armageddon."

Devotional Message:

Armageddŏn represents the ultimate confrontation between the powers of darkness and the light of Christ—a decisive battle that signals the end of the present age. This foretelling is meant to remind us that the forces of evil, no matter how formidable, are ultimately under the control of our sovereign God. It is not intended to instill panic but to galvanize believers into living with urgency and moral clarity. In the shadow of Armageddŏn, we are called to be warriors of truth, standing firm in our faith against all opposition. The imagery of this final battle encourages us to trust that justice will prevail, and that God's victory is assured. It challenges us to examine our lives, ensuring that we are on the side of righteousness and prepared for the final triumph of good. Let the promise of Armageddŏn motivate you to be steadfast and courageous in the face of spiritual adversity.

Reflection Questions for the Day:

- How does the imagery of Armageddon influence my understanding of the ultimate victory of God?
- In what ways can I prepare myself spiritually for the challenges that lie ahead?
- How can I live today as a warrior for truth in anticipation of God's final triumph?

Day 109 – θλῖψις (thlîpsis) – Tribulation

Greek Word: θλῖψις

English Word: Tribulation

Meaning: A period of severe trial, suffering, or distress that serves as both a test of faith and a refining process for believers.

Bible Reference: Matthew 24:21 – "For then there will be great tribulation, such as has not been from the beginning of the world until now, no, and never will be."

Devotional Message:

Tribulation (θλῖψις) speaks to the intense periods of hardship that believers may face in a fallen world. These times of trial are not without purpose; they are designed to test and ultimately strengthen our faith. Through tribulation, our reliance on God deepens, and our character is refined like gold in the fire. This season of suffering challenges us to remain steadfast and to trust that God is working all things for our ultimate good. Even in the midst of overwhelming difficulty, the promise of God's presence and deliverance sustains us. Tribulation teaches us resilience and patience, encouraging us to cling to the hope that our present sufferings are temporary compared to the glory that awaits. Embracing this truth enables us to face life's storms with unwavering faith, knowing that each trial brings us closer to the fullness of God's purpose.

Reflection Questions for the Day:

- How have past tribulations shaped my faith and character?
- In what ways can I lean more on God during times of severe trial?
- How does the promise of future glory motivate me to endure present hardships?

Day 110 – ἀρπαγησόμεθα (harpagēsometha) – We Shall Be Caught Up (Rapture)

Greek Word: ἀρπαγησόμεθα

English Word: We Shall Be Caught Up (Rapture)

Meaning: The promised event when believers will be taken up to meet Christ in the air, signifying their eternal union with Him.

Bible Reference: 1 Thessalonians 4:17 – "Then we who are alive, who are left, will be caught up together with them in the clouds to meet the Lord in the air."

Devotional Message:

The promise expressed in ἀρπαγησόμεθα is a source of immense hope and anticipation for believers—it assures us that one day we will be caught up to be with the Lord forever. This rapture event signifies the culmination of our earthly journey and the beginning of our eternal fellowship with Christ. It transforms our understanding of life and death, replacing fear of the end with eager expectation. The promise of being caught up together encourages us to live each day with a sense of urgency and readiness, knowing that our time on earth is temporary. It reminds us that our true home lies beyond this world and that our present struggles are but a prelude to an everlasting joy. Embracing this promise fills our hearts with comfort and motivates us to live in a manner worthy of our calling. Let this assurance inspire you to remain vigilant, faithful, and full of hope as you await the glorious return of Christ.

Reflection Questions for the Day:

- How does the promise of being caught up with the Lord shape my view of life and death?

- In what ways can I live with a sense of urgency and readiness for Christ's return?
- How does this hope impact the way I handle the challenges and uncertainties of daily life?

Day 111 – κρίσις (krísis) – Judgment

Greek Word: κρίσις
English Word: Judgment
Meaning: The divine evaluation of humanity at the end of the age, where God will render justice based on the deeds of every person.
Bible Reference: Hebrews 9:27 – "And just as it is appointed for man to die once, and after that comes judgment."

Devotional Message:

Judgment (κρίσις) is a sobering reminder that every life will be held accountable before the righteous judge, our God. It calls us to live in light of eternity, knowing that our actions have eternal consequences. This divine evaluation is not meant to instill fear, but to motivate us toward righteous living and sincere devotion to God. As we consider the certainty of judgment, we are compelled to examine our lives, confess our sins, and pursue a path of holiness. It is through the lens of judgment that we appreciate the weight of God's justice and the beauty of His mercy. Recognizing that every deed will be accounted for encourages us to live with integrity, compassion, and unwavering faith. Embracing the reality of κρίσις motivates us to share the Gospel, so others might also be saved from eternal separation.

Reflection Questions for the Day:

- How does the reality of divine judgment influence the way I live today?

- In what areas of my life do I need to seek repentance and transformation?
- How can I use the truth of God's judgment to inspire others to pursue a relationship with Him?

Day 112 – χιλιανός (chilianós) – Thousand (Millennium)

Greek Word: χιλιανός
English Word: Thousand
Meaning: In eschatological context, it often refers to a thousand-year reign, symbolizing a period of peace and divine rule on earth.
Bible Reference: Revelation 20:2-3 – "And he seized the dragon, that ancient serpent, who is the devil, and Satan, and bound him for a thousand years..."

Devotional Message:

The term χιλιανός, often associated with the millennium, symbolizes a future period of unparalleled peace and divine governance on earth. This prophetic promise offers believers a vision of a time when the forces of evil will be subdued and God's righteous rule will be fully established. It serves as both a promise and a challenge—inviting us to live in anticipation of an era marked by justice, harmony, and restored creation. The concept of a thousand-year reign encourages us to look forward to the fulfillment of God's redemptive plan and to maintain hope in the midst of current turmoil. It reminds us that God's timeline is beyond our comprehension and that His promises are sure. As we meditate on χιλιανός, we are inspired to work for peace and righteousness in our present world, knowing that a perfect future awaits. Embracing this hope motivates us to live faithfully, eagerly anticipating the day when God's Kingdom will be fully realized on earth.

Reflection Questions for the Day:

- How does the promise of a thousand-year reign of peace influence my vision for the future?
- In what ways can I contribute to the realization of God's Kingdom here and now?
- How can I hold onto hope in the midst of present challenges, knowing that a divine era of peace is promised?

Conclusion – Eschatology (End Times)

Throughout this week, we have journeyed through some of the most profound and mysterious aspects of eschatology, discovering a tapestry of promises and warnings about the end times. We began with ἀποκάλυψις, where God reveals His divine plan to bring history to its ultimate climax. The promise of Christ's παρουσία fills us with hope as we await His glorious return, while Ἀρμαγεδδών reminds us of the decisive battle that will usher in God's righteous victory. The reality of θλῖψις calls us to endure hardship with steadfast faith, knowing that our suffering is but a prelude to future glory. The promise of ἁρπαγησόμεθα assures us of our eternal union with Christ, and the truth of κρίσις urges us to live with accountability and purpose. Finally, the vision of χιλιανός gives us a glimpse of the future era of peace and divine rule that awaits the faithful. Collectively, these truths compel us to live with urgency, hope, and unwavering commitment, ever mindful of the eternal perspective that shapes our lives. May these reflections inspire us to remain faithful, prepared, and ever watchful as we await the fulfillment of God's magnificent plan.

Reflection Questions for the Week:

- How has studying eschatological promises and warnings affected my perspective on daily life?

- What steps can I take to live with greater readiness and faithfulness in light of these truths?
- In what ways does the hope of Christ's return influence my decisions and priorities?
- How can I encourage others to understand the eternal significance of our present struggles?
- What areas of my heart need renewal as I anticipate the fulfillment of God's promises?
- How does the promise of a future era of peace motivate me to work for righteousness today?

Week 17: Missions and Evangelism.

Missions and Evangelism: The Call to Share the Gospel

Missions and evangelism are at the heart of Christ's command to His followers. Before ascending to heaven, Jesus gave the Great Commission in **Matthew 28:19-20**: *"Go therefore and make disciples of all nations, baptizing them in the name of the Father and of the Son and of the Holy Spirit, teaching them to observe all that I have commanded you."* This mission is not for a select few but for every believer, as we are all called to share the Good News of salvation.

Evangelism is not just about preaching—it is about living a life that reflects Christ's love and truth. Whether through words, acts of kindness, or simply being a light in our communities, we are witnesses of His grace. Missions extend beyond our local surroundings, reaching the lost across the world, ensuring that every person has the opportunity to hear and respond to the Gospel.

We do not share the Gospel in our own strength but through the power of the Holy Spirit (Acts 1:8). The harvest is plentiful, and God is calling us to labor faithfully. Let us boldly proclaim Christ, knowing that every effort to share His love has eternal significance in bringing people into His Kingdom.

Day 113 – μαθητεύω (mathētéuō) – To Make Disciples

Greek Word: μαθητεύω
English Word: To Make Disciples
Meaning: To train, instruct, and lead others into a personal relationship with Christ, guiding them to follow His teachings and example.

Bible Reference: Matthew 28:19 – "Go therefore and make disciples of all nations..."

Devotional Message:

To μαθητεύω is to take seriously the Great Commission by intentionally investing in the spiritual growth of others. It calls us to step beyond our comfort zones and actively engage in sharing Christ's love with those who have not yet experienced His saving grace. As we make disciples, we not only teach biblical truths but also model a lifestyle of faith, demonstrating how to live in obedience to God's Word. This process requires patience, persistence, and a genuine love for others—qualities that are cultivated through prayer, study, and dependence on the Holy Spirit. By discipling others, we participate in God's redemptive work on earth and extend His kingdom. Each conversation and mentoring moment becomes an opportunity to reflect Christ's heart. Embracing μαθητεύω reminds us that our lives are intertwined with the destiny of others, calling us to be active partners in God's mission.

Reflection Questions for the Day:

- In what practical ways can I invest in the spiritual growth of someone around me?
- How can I model Christ-like behavior as I disciple others?
- What challenges do I face when sharing my faith, and how might I overcome them through prayer and reliance on the Holy Spirit?

Day 114 – κηρύσσω (kērússō) – To Preach/Proclaim

Greek Word: κηρύσσω
English Word: To Preach/Proclaim
Meaning: To announce or declare the Gospel of Jesus Christ boldly,

making His message known to all.

Bible Reference: Mark 16:15 – "Go into all the world and proclaim the gospel to the whole creation."

Devotional Message:

The act of κηρύσσω compels us to share the transformative message of the Gospel without hesitation or compromise. It involves not only speaking the truth but also living it out in such a way that others are drawn to Christ. Proclaiming the Gospel is both a duty and a privilege—it is our response to God's call to be His witnesses. Through our words and actions, we shine the light of Christ into dark places, offering hope and salvation to those in need. This calling requires boldness, clarity, and a deep reliance on the guidance of the Holy Spirit. As we step forward to preach the good news, we become living instruments of God's grace and mercy. Embracing κηρύσσω challenges us to overcome fear, trust in God's power, and be unashamed of the message that has changed our lives.

Reflection Questions for the Day:

- What specific opportunities do I have today to proclaim the Gospel?
- How can I overcome my fears of sharing my faith with others?
- In what ways can my life serve as a testimony to the truth of the Gospel?

Day 115 – μαρτυρία (martyría) – Testimony/Witness

Greek Word: μαρτυρία
English Word: Testimony/Witness
Meaning: The act of bearing witness to the truth of the Gospel through one's life, experiences, and personal encounters with

Christ.

Bible Reference: Acts 1:8 – "But you will receive power when the Holy Spirit has come upon you, and you will be my witnesses (μαρτυρία)..."

Devotional Message:

Μαρτυρία is the sharing of our personal encounter with Jesus— telling the story of how His love, sacrifice, and resurrection have transformed our lives. Our testimony is a powerful tool that connects others with the reality of God's grace. It is not just about words; it is the living evidence of change that radiates from a heart touched by Christ. When we share our witness, we affirm that the Gospel is not a set of abstract doctrines but a dynamic force that brings hope and renewal. Our stories of transformation serve to inspire faith in others and build bridges to the Gospel. Embracing μαρτυρία means being courageous in revealing both our struggles and our victories, knowing that God can use our weaknesses to showcase His strength. Let your life be a radiant testimony that points others to the saving power of Christ.

Reflection Questions for the Day:

- What is the most compelling aspect of my testimony that reflects God's work in my life?
- How can I share my story in a way that is both honest and hopeful?
- In what ways does my witness encourage others to seek a relationship with Christ?

Day 116 – μαθητής (mathētḗs) – Disciple

Greek Word: μαθητής
English Word: Disciple
Meaning: A follower of Christ who learns from His teachings and

imitates His lifestyle, committed to growth in faith.

Bible Reference: Luke 14:27 – "Whoever does not carry his own cross and follow me cannot be my disciple."

Devotional Message:

Being a μαθητής involves more than just professing faith—it means actively following Jesus and committing to a life of continuous learning and transformation. As disciples, we are called to adopt Christ's teachings, embrace His example, and dedicate ourselves to living out the principles of His Kingdom. This journey requires discipline, humility, and a willingness to be challenged and changed by God's Word. It is through the daily practice of obedience, prayer, and fellowship that we grow as disciples. Our lives become a living classroom where every experience teaches us more about God's love, mercy, and truth. Embracing discipleship means walking in step with Christ, even when the path is difficult, and trusting that He is continually shaping us into His image. In being a disciple, we are not only transformed ourselves but also equipped to lead others into the fullness of God's grace.

Reflection Questions for the Day:

- In what areas of my life do I need to grow more as a disciple of Christ?
- How can I better align my daily actions with the teachings of Jesus?
- What practices can I adopt to ensure continuous spiritual growth and learning?

Day 117 – πρεσβεύω (presbeúō) – To Be an Ambassador

Greek Word: πρεσβεύω
English Word: To Be an Ambassador
Meaning: To represent Christ to the world, acting as a

spokesperson and representative of His love and truth.

Bible Reference: 2 Corinthians 5:20 – "Therefore, we are ambassadors for Christ, God making his appeal through us."

Devotional Message:

Το πρεσβεύω is to accept the profound responsibility of representing Jesus to every person we encounter. As ambassadors, we carry not only the message of the Gospel but also the very character of Christ, reflecting His love, mercy, and truth in all our interactions. This calling demands that our words and actions align with the principles of the Kingdom, serving as a living bridge between a hurting world and a Savior who offers hope. When we embrace this role, we become conduits of God's grace, entrusted with the mission to reconcile others to Him. Our lives then speak louder than words, as we model integrity, compassion, and courage in sharing the Good News. The ambassadorial duty challenges us to be proactive in our witness, engaging with both believers and non-believers alike. Embracing this identity transforms every encounter into an opportunity to extend the love of Christ and invite others into a relationship with Him.

Reflection Questions for the Day:

- How am I currently representing Christ in my daily interactions?
- What changes can I make to better reflect His character as His ambassador?
- In what ways can I actively share the Gospel with those who have yet to experience His love?

Day 118 – ἀπόστολος (apóstolos) – Apostle

Greek Word: ἀπόστολος

English Word: Apostle

Meaning: One who is sent out with a special commission to spread the Gospel, often characterized by a pioneering spirit and sacrificial service.

Bible Reference: Romans 1:1 – "Paul, a servant of Christ Jesus, called to be an apostle, set apart for the gospel of God..."

Devotional Message:

The term ἀπόστολος signifies a messenger uniquely commissioned by Christ to establish and expand His Kingdom. Apostles were chosen not only for their faith but for their willingness to endure hardship and sacrifice for the sake of the Gospel. As modern believers, we may not all hold the title of "apostle" in the traditional sense, yet we are all sent out with a divine mandate to proclaim the Good News. Embracing this calling involves stepping out with boldness, trusting that God equips those He sends. It is a life marked by purpose, where every word and deed points others toward Christ. The apostolic mission challenges us to be pioneers in our communities, laying a foundation of faith that endures through generations. Let the spirit of an ἀπόστολος inspire you to live courageously and to share the Gospel with unwavering passion.

Reflection Questions for the Day:

- In what ways am I being sent out as an ambassador for the Gospel in my community?
- How can I better embrace the apostolic call to pioneer new avenues of faith?
- What sacrifices am I willing to make to further the spread of Christ's message?

Day 119 – εὐαγγελίζω (euangelízō) – To Evangelize

Greek Word: εὐαγγελίζω

English Word: To Evangelize

Meaning: To actively proclaim the good news of Jesus Christ, inviting others to experience His salvation and transforming love.

Bible Reference: Luke 4:18 – "The Spirit of the Lord is upon me, because he has anointed me to proclaim good news (εὐαγγελίζω) to the poor..."

Devotional Message:

Το εὐαγγελίζω is to joyfully share the life-changing message of the Gospel with a world in desperate need of hope. Evangelism is not merely about conversion; it is about inviting others into a personal relationship with Jesus and demonstrating His love through compassionate action. This calling challenges us to step out of our comfort zones, engage in heartfelt conversations, and meet people where they are. When we evangelize, we participate in God's redemptive plan, planting seeds of faith that can grow into vibrant communities of believers. It is an act of love that requires sensitivity, persistence, and reliance on the Holy Spirit for guidance. As we share the good news, we become channels of divine hope, witnessing to the transformative power of Christ's grace.

Embracing εὐαγγελίζω means committing ourselves to a lifestyle of outreach, where every interaction becomes an opportunity to introduce someone to the Savior.

Reflection Questions for the Day:

- What practical steps can I take to share the Gospel with those around me?
- How can I overcome my fears or hesitations about evangelizing?

- In what ways can my personal testimony serve as a powerful tool for sharing the good news of Jesus?

Conclusion – Missions and Evangelism

Throughout this week, we have journeyed through the various aspects of God's mission in the world, discovering the multifaceted call to spread His Gospel. We began with μαθητεύω, emphasizing the importance of making disciples through intentional, loving mentorship. Our exploration of κηρύσσω challenged us to boldly proclaim the Gospel in both word and deed. In sharing our μαρτυρία, we learned that our personal stories of transformation serve as powerful testimonies of God's redeeming love. As disciples (μαθητής) of Christ, we are invited to follow His example daily and embrace a life of obedience and growth. Our call to act as ambassadors (πρεσβεύω) reminds us that every believer has a unique role in representing Christ to the world, while the apostolic call (ἀπόστολος) encourages us to pioneer new paths in the mission field. Finally, our commitment to εὐαγγελίζω encapsulates the joy and urgency of sharing the Good News with everyone. Collectively, these truths reveal that missions and evangelism are not distant, abstract concepts but practical, daily commitments that shape our identity as followers of Christ. May the insights from this week inspire us to live boldly for the Gospel, to invest in the spiritual growth of others, and to continually share the hope we have in Jesus with a world in need.

Reflection Questions for the Week:

- How does my understanding of missions and evangelism impact my daily interactions and priorities?
- What steps can I take to be more intentional in making disciples and sharing the Gospel?

- In what ways can I strengthen my personal testimony to better reflect the transformative power of Christ?
- How can I support and encourage others who are called to be ambassadors and evangelists in their communities?
- What specific actions will I commit to this week to advance God's mission in my sphere of influence?
- How does embracing the call to be an apostle, in the sense of being a bold messenger for Christ, change my approach to challenges?
- In what ways can I cultivate a spirit of evangelism that is both loving and courageous, inspiring those around me to know Christ?

Week 18: Christian Living.

Christian Living: Walking in the Light of Christ

Christian living is more than just believing in Jesus—it is about following Him daily in obedience, love, and faith. **Galatians 2:20** says, *"I have been crucified with Christ. It is no longer I who live, but Christ who lives in me."* When we accept Christ, our lives are transformed, and we are called to reflect His character in everything we do.

Living as a Christian means walking in righteousness, loving others, and striving for holiness. It requires a commitment to prayer, studying God's Word, and seeking His will above our own. The Bible calls us to be **"doers of the word, and not hearers only"** (James 1:22), meaning our faith must be evident in our actions. Whether in our relationships, work, or daily choices, we should seek to glorify God in all things (1 Corinthians 10:31).

Christian living is not always easy, but God gives us His Spirit to guide and strengthen us. As we grow in faith, we experience the peace, joy, and purpose that come from walking with Him. Let us daily strive to live as Christ's disciples, shining His light in a world that desperately needs His truth and love.

Day 120 – περιπατέω (peripatéō) – Walk

Greek Word: περιπατέω
English Word: Walk
Meaning: To live or conduct oneself in a manner that reflects one's faith; to follow Christ's example in every step of life.
Bible Reference: Ephesians 4:1 – "I therefore, a prisoner for the Lord, urge you to walk in a manner worthy of the calling to which you have been called."

Devotional Message:

Walking (περιπατέω) as a follower of Christ means more than simply moving through life; it is about the manner in which we live each day. Our walk is a visible testimony of our commitment to live according to God's Word. Every decision, action, and interaction becomes a step along the path of righteousness. When we walk in a manner worthy of our calling, we mirror the humility, love, and integrity of Christ. This daily journey calls us to be intentional—choosing the narrow path that leads to eternal life over the broad way that leads to destruction. It challenges us to reflect on our motives, aligning them with God's truth and grace. As you walk each day, let your steps be guided by the Spirit, knowing that God is with you every step of the way.

Reflection Questions for the Day:

- In what practical ways can I ensure my daily walk reflects my calling in Christ?
- How do my actions at work, home, or in the community serve as a testimony to my faith?
- What changes can I make today to align my life more closely with God's standards?

Day 121 – ἄξιος (áxios) – Worthy

Greek Word: ἄξιος

English Word: Worthy

Meaning: Deserving honor, value, or reward; reflecting the character and dignity that comes from living a life approved by God.

Bible Reference: Philippians 1:27 – "Only let your manner of life be worthy of the gospel of Christ…"

Devotional Message:

To be ἄξιος means to live in a way that is honorable and pleasing before God. It is a call to demonstrate through our character and conduct that we are valuable as God's children. This worthiness is not earned by our own efforts but is rooted in our identity in Christ; however, our actions serve as a reflection of that identity. Living worthily involves striving for excellence in all we do—honoring God with our time, talents, and resources. It challenges us to pursue integrity, humility, and compassion in every circumstance. As we walk in worthiness, we become a beacon of light, inspiring others to seek the same quality of life that comes from a deep relationship with Jesus. Let every decision and every act be a declaration that you are indeed worthy to represent the gospel.

Reflection Questions for the Day:

- How does my current lifestyle reflect my worthiness as a child of God?
- In what ways can I further honor God in my daily actions?
- How can I encourage others to live in a manner worthy of the gospel?

Day 122 – μιμέομαι (miméomai) – Imitate

Greek Word: μιμέομαι
English Word: Imitate
Meaning: To follow as a pattern or example; to mirror the character and actions of someone, especially Christ.
Bible Reference: 1 Corinthians 11:1 – "Be imitators of me, as I am of Christ."

Devotional Message:

To μιμέομαι is to actively follow the example set by those who have walked faithfully before us, with Christ as our ultimate model.

Imitation in the Christian life means not merely copying actions but embracing the heart, attitude, and values that defined Jesus' life. It challenges us to examine our own behaviors, striving to reflect His humility, compassion, and truth in every situation. When we choose to imitate Christ, we open ourselves to transformation as His character begins to shine through our own lives. This process requires intentionality—regular prayer, reflection on Scripture, and a willingness to be shaped by the examples of godly mentors. As we imitate the best of what Christ has shown us, our lives become living sermons, drawing others to the love and grace of our Savior. Let your life be a mirror reflecting the light of Christ to a world in need.

Reflection Questions for the Day:

- In what areas of my life can I better imitate the character of Christ?
- Who in my community exemplifies Christ-like behavior, and how can I learn from them?
- What habits or attitudes do I need to change in order to more fully reflect Jesus' example?

Day 123 – νέος ἄνθρωπος (néos ánthrōpos) – New Self

Greek Word: νέος ἄνθρωπος

English Word: New Self

Meaning: The renewed, transformed identity of a believer in Christ, characterized by righteousness and a departure from the old way of life.

Bible Reference: 2 Corinthians 5:17 – "Therefore, if anyone is in Christ, he is a new creation. The old has passed away; behold, the new has come."

Devotional Message:

Embracing the νέος ἄνθρωπος means stepping into the new life that God has graciously given us through Christ's sacrifice. Our old ways, marred by sin and separation from God, are replaced by a renewed identity that reflects His glory. This transformation is not superficial but penetrates every area of our being—mind, heart, and actions. Living as a new self involves daily surrender to God's transforming power, allowing the Holy Spirit to reshape our thoughts, desires, and priorities. It calls us to reject the patterns of the past and to embrace a lifestyle that is centered on Christ's teachings and love. Our new self is a testimony to God's redemptive work in our lives, and it serves as a powerful witness to others. Let the reality of being a new creation empower you to live boldly and authentically for the glory of God.

Reflection Questions for the Day:

- How has my identity in Christ transformed my thoughts and actions?
- What aspects of my old self do I still need to surrender to God?
- In what ways can I more clearly demonstrate the reality of my new creation to those around me?

Day 124 – νηφάω (nēpháō) – Be Sober

Greek Word: νηφάω
English Word: Be Sober
Meaning: To remain self-controlled, alert, and clear-minded, particularly in spiritual matters; to be watchful and vigilant.
Bible Reference: 1 Peter 5:8 – "Be sober-minded; be watchful. Your adversary the devil prowls around like a roaring lion..."

Devotional Message:

To νηφάω is to embrace a lifestyle of vigilance and self-control, ensuring that our minds and hearts remain focused on God's truth. Being sober-minded is not solely about physical sobriety, but more importantly, about maintaining spiritual clarity and discipline. In a world filled with distractions and temptations, sobriety helps us to discern God's voice and to respond with wisdom. This alertness is essential for resisting the subtle attacks of the enemy and for living in accordance with God's will. A sober mind is one that is anchored in Scripture, prayer, and the fellowship of believers, continually refreshed by the Holy Spirit. As we practice sobriety, we develop a heightened sensitivity to God's presence and a resilient spirit that is prepared for whatever challenges may come. Let your life reflect the clarity and focus that come from walking in God's light.

Reflection Questions for the Day:

- What distractions or habits do I need to eliminate to better maintain spiritual alertness?
- How can I cultivate greater self-control and focus in my daily life?
- In what ways can I stay connected to God's truth throughout the busyness of my day?

Day 125 – ἀναστροφή (anastrophḗ) – Conduct/Way of Life

Greek Word: ἀναστροφή
English Word: Conduct/Way of Life
Meaning: The manner in which one lives, characterized by actions that honor God and reflect a transformed heart.
Bible Reference: 1 Peter 1:15 – "But as he who called you is holy, you also be holy in all your conduct (ἀναστροφή)."

Devotional Message:

The term ἀναστροφή speaks to the overall conduct and lifestyle that we adopt as followers of Christ. It is the outward expression of our inward transformation, the way we carry ourselves in every interaction and decision. Living a godly conduct means aligning our behavior with the holiness of God and allowing His love to guide our actions. It calls us to a consistency where our private devotion mirrors our public life, and our values are evident in every facet of our existence. This way of life requires constant self-reflection, repentance, and the continual renewal of our minds by God's Word. As we cultivate a lifestyle that honors Him, we become a living testimony to the transformative power of the Gospel.

Embrace ἀναστροφή as a daily commitment to live in a manner that is pleasing to God and edifying to others.

Reflection Questions for the Day:

- How does my daily conduct reflect my commitment to living a holy life?
- In what areas of my life do I need to align my actions more closely with God's standards?
- What practical steps can I take today to ensure that my lifestyle is a true reflection of my faith?

Day 126 – καρποφορέω (karpophoréō) – Bear Fruit

Greek Word: καρποφορέω
English Word: Bear Fruit
Meaning: To produce visible evidence of spiritual growth and maturity through good works and righteous living.
Bible Reference: Colossians 1:10 – "...so as to walk in a manner worthy of the Lord, fully pleasing to him, bearing fruit in every good work and increasing in the knowledge of God."

Devotional Message:

Το καρποφορέω is to live in such a way that the evidence of our faith is clear for all to see. Bearing fruit means that our lives produce the kind of good works that glorify God and uplift those around us. This fruit is not accidental but is the natural outcome of a heart transformed by the Gospel and nurtured by the Holy Spirit. As we grow in spiritual maturity, we become more effective in reflecting the character of Christ in our actions and interactions. Bearing fruit serves as a testimony to others, demonstrating that a life surrendered to God leads to a tangible impact in the world. It challenges us to pursue excellence in every area, using our gifts and talents to benefit our community and further God's kingdom. Let your life be marked by abundant fruit, a living witness to the power and grace of God at work within you.

Reflection Questions for the Day:

- In what specific ways is my life bearing fruit that reflects my relationship with Christ?
- What areas of spiritual growth do I need to cultivate further to produce more fruit?
- How can I actively use my gifts to serve others and glorify God?

Conclusion – Christian Living

Throughout this week, we have explored the essential elements of Christian living that define our daily walk with God. We began by examining περιπατέω, reminding us that every step we take should reflect our commitment to follow Christ. Being ἄξιος challenged us to live honorably, while μιμέομαι urged us to imitate the very example of Jesus in all we do. Embracing our identity as a νέος ἄνθρωπος transformed our understanding of who we are in Christ, calling us to leave behind our old ways. Practicing νηφάω helped us maintain spiritual clarity and vigilance, and ἀναστροφή called us to conduct ourselves in a manner that is pleasing to God. Finally, by bearing fruit (καρποφορέω), we manifest the visible results of a life transformed by the Gospel. Collectively, these truths shape a vibrant picture of what it means to live as a follower of Christ every day. May we commit ourselves to this lifestyle, continually growing in our relationship with God and radiating His love to the world around us.

Reflection Questions for the Week:

- How has each aspect of Christian living discussed this week impacted my daily walk with God?
- What specific changes can I make in my lifestyle to more clearly reflect my identity in Christ?
- In what ways can I further cultivate spiritual disciplines that enhance my growth and witness?
- How can I use my actions and attitudes to serve as a living testimony of the Gospel?
- What areas of my life still need transformation so that I may bear more fruit for God?
- How can I encourage and support others in their journey of Christian living?
- What commitments will I make this week to ensure that my lifestyle consistently honors God in every way?

Week 19: Trials and Persecution.

Trials and Persecution: Strengthened Through Faith

Trials and persecution are inevitable for those who follow Christ. **Jesus warned in John 16:33**, *"In the world you will have tribulation. But take heart; I have overcome the world."* Challenges, suffering, and even opposition for our faith are not signs of God's absence but opportunities to grow deeper in Him.

James 1:2-3 encourages us to *"count it all joy when you meet trials of various kinds, for you know that the testing of your faith produces steadfastness."* Every trial refines our faith, strengthens our character, and draws us closer to God. While persecution can be painful, we are reminded that Christ Himself suffered rejection, humiliation, and death, yet He remained faithful to His mission.

The apostle Paul reminds us that nothing—neither hardship, distress, nor persecution—can separate us from the love of Christ (Romans 8:35-39). When we endure trials, we are not alone; the Holy Spirit sustains us, and the reward of faithfulness is eternal. Instead of fearing difficulties, let us trust in God's sovereign plan, knowing that our perseverance brings Him glory. As we stand firm in trials, we become living testimonies of His grace and strength to a world in need of hope.

Day 127 – δοκιμή (dokimḗ) – Proven Character

Greek Word: δοκιμή
English Word: Proven Character
Meaning: The testing or trial of one's faith and character, which refines and confirms our spiritual maturity.
Bible Reference: Romans 5:4 – "And endurance produces character, and character produces hope."

Devotional Message:

The word δοκιμή reminds us that trials are not meaningless difficulties but purposeful tests that refine our inner character. As we face various challenges, our faith is put to the test, revealing the depth of our trust in God. These tests are opportunities for growth, as enduring hardship produces a character that is resilient and full of hope. When our character is proven through trials, we become living testimonies of God's transforming work in our lives. Even when the process is painful, it is God's way of strengthening us and preparing us for greater responsibilities in His kingdom. The refining process of δοκιμή teaches us to depend less on our own strength and more on the sustaining power of Christ. Embracing these trials, we learn that our struggles ultimately lead to spiritual maturity and an enduring hope that cannot be shaken.

Reflection Questions for the Day:

- How have recent trials contributed to refining my character?
- What lessons can I learn from the tests I have experienced in my faith?
- In what ways can I lean more on God during times of trial?

Day 128 – πειρασμός (peirasmós) – Temptation/Test

Greek Word: πειρασμός
English Word: Temptation/Test
Meaning: The experience of being tempted or tested, which challenges our commitment and reliance on God.
Bible Reference: James 1:2-3 – "Count it all joy, my brothers, when you meet trials of various kinds, for you know that the testing of your faith produces steadfastness."

Devotional Message:

Πειρασμός speaks to the moments when we are lured or challenged to stray from our walk with God. These temptations are not only obstacles but also opportunities for growth in our faith, teaching us the value of perseverance. In facing temptation, we learn to discern between the fleeting allure of sin and the eternal rewards of living according to God's will. Each test of faith is a chance to fortify our spiritual resolve and to practice relying on God's strength rather than our own. Though temptation can feel overwhelming, it is often a gateway through which God refines our character and draws us closer to Him. Embracing these challenges with a joyful spirit can transform our perspective, making us more resilient and more attuned to the guidance of the Holy Spirit. Let every encounter with temptation be an opportunity to affirm your commitment to Christ and to grow in spiritual maturity.

Reflection Questions for the Day:

- What temptations have challenged my faith recently, and how have I responded?
- In what ways can I better rely on God to overcome trials of temptation?
- How can I view these tests as opportunities for spiritual growth and endurance?

Day 129 – διωγμός (diōgmós) – Persecution

Greek Word: διωγμός
English Word: Persecution
Meaning: The suffering, hostility, or oppression directed toward believers because of their faith in Christ.
Bible Reference: 2 Timothy 3:12 – "Indeed, all who desire to live a godly life in Christ Jesus will be persecuted."

Devotional Message:

Διωγμός encapsulates the reality that following Christ often comes with facing hostility and oppression from the world. Persecution is not a sign of divine abandonment but a profound indicator that we are living in truth and standing firm in our faith. The sufferings we experience for the sake of the Gospel connect us with the early believers and with Christ Himself, who endured much on our behalf. In the face of persecution, our commitment to Christ is strengthened, and our resolve to live out His truth becomes even more evident. These challenges refine our testimony, making us bold witnesses of God's grace despite adversity. Persecution invites us to draw nearer to God, finding comfort in His promise that He is always with us even in the darkest moments. Let every act of persecution serve as a reminder of our heavenly reward and the eternal hope that sustains us.

Reflection Questions for the Day:

- How has experiencing persecution deepened my faith and reliance on God?
- In what ways can I find encouragement during times of hostility or oppression?
- How can my response to persecution serve as a powerful testimony to others?

Day 130 – κακουχέομαι (kakouchéomai) – Suffer Hardship

Greek Word: κακουχέομαι
English Word: Suffer Hardship
Meaning: To endure difficulty or affliction, often as a part of the refining process of faith.
Bible Reference: Hebrews 11:37 – "They were well reported, indeed, for their faith, yet suffering through torture and imprisonment."

Devotional Message:

The term κακουχέομαι speaks to the experience of enduring severe hardships and trials that test the limits of our strength. These hardships, though painful, are a part of the journey of faith that God uses to mold and refine us. Through suffering, we gain a deeper understanding of our dependence on God and learn to trust in His sustaining grace. It is in these moments of profound difficulty that the reality of our faith is both tested and strengthened. Suffering hardship can lead to a richer, more compassionate life, as we come to identify with the struggles of others. This process also reveals the beauty of God's redemptive power, turning even our darkest moments into opportunities for spiritual growth. Embracing hardship as part of God's refining work empowers us to face future challenges with courage and unwavering trust in His purpose.

Reflection Questions for the Day:

- What hardships have I endured that have ultimately strengthened my faith?
- How can I view current difficulties as opportunities for growth and refinement?
- In what ways can I support others who are experiencing similar trials?

Day 131 – Ὑπομένω (hypoménō) – To Endure

Greek Word: ὑπομένω

English Word: To Endure

Meaning: To persevere or remain steadfast under difficult circumstances, holding on to hope and faith.

Bible Reference: 2 Timothy 2:10 – "Therefore I endure everything for the sake of the elect, that they also may obtain the salvation that is in Christ Jesus."

Devotional Message:

Ὑπομένω calls us to a steadfast perseverance in the face of all challenges, encouraging us to hold on to our faith despite adversity. Endurance is not merely about surviving trials—it is about growing stronger in character and spirit as we continue to trust God. Through enduring hardship, we develop a resilience that equips us for future challenges and deepens our understanding of God's unwavering love. This perseverance is powered by hope and sustained by prayer, allowing us to overcome obstacles that might otherwise break our spirit. When we endure, we become living testimonies of God's grace and the transformative power of faith.

Embracing ὑπομένω means acknowledging that while we may face significant challenges, our ultimate victory is secured in Christ. Let your endurance be a beacon of hope to others, demonstrating that with God's help, we can overcome even the most daunting trials.

Reflection Questions for the Day:

- What does it mean to me to endure in my personal walk with God?
- How have moments of endurance shaped my character and deepened my faith?
- What strategies can I adopt to maintain hope and perseverance during challenging times?

Day 132 – παθήματα (pathémata) – Sufferings

Greek Word: παθήματα
English Word: Sufferings
Meaning: The experiences of pain, affliction, or distress that

believers encounter as part of their earthly journey.

Bible Reference: 1 Peter 5:10 – "And after you have suffered a little while, the God of all grace, who has called you to his eternal glory in Christ, will himself restore, confirm, strengthen, and establish you."

Devotional Message:

Παθήματα encapsulates the various sufferings and challenges that are a part of our human experience, especially for those who follow Christ. These sufferings, though painful, are not without purpose; they are instruments through which God refines our faith and prepares us for His glory. In our moments of distress, we are invited to lean on God's promises and to trust that He is working all things for our good. The trials we endure serve as both a test and a testimony—demonstrating that our hope is not in the absence of pain but in the presence of a loving God who sustains us. As we face our sufferings, we are reminded that they are temporary and that a glorious future awaits those who remain faithful. Embracing our παθήματα allows us to grow in empathy, understanding, and reliance on the Holy Spirit. Let our experiences of suffering ultimately point us toward the hope of restoration and the promise of eternal joy.

Reflection Questions for the Day:

- How have my sufferings contributed to my spiritual growth and understanding of God's grace?
- In what ways can I use my experiences of pain to offer comfort and hope to others?
- How can I remain hopeful and trusting during times of intense distress?

Day 133 – στενοχωρία (stenochōría) – Distress

Greek Word: στενοχωρία

English Word: Distress

Meaning: A state of deep sorrow, anxiety, or discomfort, often resulting from trials and hardships.

Bible Reference: Romans 8:35 – "Who shall separate us from the love of Christ? Shall tribulation (στενοχωρία), or distress..."

Devotional Message:

Στενοχωρία captures the overwhelming sense of sorrow or anxiety that can grip our hearts during times of trial. It is a reminder that distress is a natural part of the human experience, yet even in our deepest moments of pain, we are not abandoned by God. In the midst of distress, we are called to seek refuge in the love and comfort of Christ, who promises to be with us through every storm. This distress, while painful, also deepens our reliance on God and opens our eyes to His sustaining grace. As we experience these moments, we are invited to cast our cares on Him, knowing that His love is greater than any trouble we may face. Embracing στενοχωρία means acknowledging our vulnerability while also clinging to the hope that God will deliver us. Let your distress become a catalyst for drawing closer to God, finding solace and strength in His unwavering presence.

Reflection Questions for the Day:

- What sources of distress do I encounter most frequently, and how can I bring them before God?
- In what ways can I experience God's comfort during times of deep anxiety?
- How can I turn my moments of distress into opportunities for spiritual growth and reliance on God?

Conclusion – Trials and Persecution

Throughout this week, we have journeyed through the challenging yet refining aspects of trials and persecution. We began by understanding δοκιμή as the testing that produces proven character and hope. In facing πειρασμός, we learned that temptations are opportunities for growth when met with faith. Our exploration of διωγμός highlighted that persecution, though painful, is a sign that we are living out the truth of the Gospel. We then delved into κακουχέομαι and ὑπομένω, learning that enduring hardship and persevering in faith fortify our spiritual resilience. Our reflection on παθήματα and στενοχωρία brought home the reality that suffering and distress, while deeply challenging, serve to draw us closer to God's compassionate presence. Collectively, these experiences remind us that trials and persecution are not signs of defeat but opportunities for divine refinement and ultimate victory in Christ. May the insights of this week inspire you to face each challenge with courage, trust in God's sustaining grace, and continue to stand firm in your faith.

Reflection Questions for the Week:

- How have the trials and persecutions I've experienced shaped my spiritual character?
- In what ways can I view temptations and distress as opportunities for growth and reliance on God?
- How does understanding the purpose of suffering encourage me to endure hardships with hope?
- What practical steps can I take to cultivate perseverance in the face of adversity?
- How can I support fellow believers who are experiencing persecution and trials?
- In what ways has God's promise of restoration and strength sustained me during difficult times?
- What commitments will I make to remain faithful and resilient, even in the midst of suffering?

Week 20: Sanctification.

Sanctification: Growing in Holiness

Sanctification is the process of becoming more like Christ, set apart for God's purpose. It is not a one-time event but a lifelong journey of spiritual growth. **1 Thessalonians 4:3** declares, *"For this is the will of God, your sanctification: that you abstain from sexual immorality."* God desires for us to live holy lives, reflecting His righteousness in our thoughts, actions, and character.

This transformation is the work of the Holy Spirit, who renews our hearts and minds as we surrender to God's will (Romans 12:2). Through prayer, Scripture, and obedience, we grow in grace, learning to walk in the Spirit rather than the flesh. Though we may struggle with sin, sanctification assures us that God is continually shaping us, refining our faith, and strengthening our character.

Sanctification is not about perfection but about progress—daily becoming more aligned with Christ's image. It requires discipline, perseverance, and dependence on God's power. As we yield to Him, He purifies us, making us vessels for His glory (2 Timothy 2:21). Let us embrace sanctification as a privilege, knowing that God is molding us into the people He created us to be for His kingdom.

Day 134 – ἁγιασμός (hagiasmós) – Sanctification

Greek Word: ἁγιασμός

English Word: Sanctification

Meaning: The process of being set apart from sin and dedicated to God's purposes; a lifelong journey of becoming holy.

Bible Reference: 1 Thessalonians 4:3 – "For this is the will of God, your sanctification..."

Devotional Message:

Sanctification is God's transformative work in our lives, separating us from sin and setting us apart for His service. As we yield to His refining process, we are gradually molded into the image of Christ. Every trial, every moment of obedience, and every act of surrender contributes to this sacred transformation. God's sanctifying work is not instantaneous but a lifelong journey of continual renewal and growth. It calls us to daily repentance, prayer, and an earnest desire to reflect His character. Embracing sanctification means allowing the Holy Spirit to change our hearts and minds, producing a life that honors God in every detail. Let this process remind you that your journey toward holiness is both a privilege and a calling from a loving Father.

Reflection Questions for the Day:

- In what ways have I seen God at work sanctifying my life?
- How can I better yield to His transforming process in my daily walk?
- What specific areas of my life need further refinement and surrender to God's will?

Day 135 – ἅγιος (hágios) – Holy

Greek Word: ἅγιος
English Word: Holy
Meaning: Set apart for God; characterized by purity, righteousness, and divine purpose.
Bible Reference: 1 Peter 1:16 – "Be holy, for I am holy."

Devotional Message:

To be called holy means to be separated from the corruption of the world and dedicated to God's service. The call to holiness is not based on our own strength but on the transforming power of Christ in our lives. As we strive to live in holiness, our thoughts, words, and actions begin to mirror the character of our Savior. This pursuit of holiness invites us to reject sin and embrace a lifestyle that honors God. It is a daily commitment to aligning our will with His, and to reflecting His light in a dark world. Living a holy life is both a privilege and a responsibility, as it testifies to the power of God's grace at work in us. May we continually seek to be set apart, not for our own glory, but for the glory of our Heavenly Father.

Reflection Questions for the Day:

- What does living a holy life look like in my everyday actions?
- How can I better reflect the character of Christ to those around me?
- In what ways can I set aside distractions that pull me away from pursuing holiness?

Day 136 – καθαρός (katharós) – Clean/Pure

Greek Word: καθαρός
English Word: Clean/Pure
Meaning: Free from moral or spiritual defilement; characterized by integrity and a heart devoted to God.
Bible Reference: Matthew 5:8 – "Blessed are the pure in heart, for they shall see God."

Devotional Message:

Being καθαρός calls us to a state of purity that touches every part of our lives—our thoughts, our actions, and our relationships. This purity is not merely about outward appearances but involves an inner cleanliness that comes from a surrendered heart. When God purifies us, He removes the stains of sin and fills us with His light, enabling us to see and reflect His glory. The pursuit of purity is a continuous journey that requires diligence, prayer, and a willingness to turn away from anything that compromises our integrity. As we walk in purity, we become clearer channels of God's truth and love, shining as beacons of hope in a troubled world. Embracing a life of purity brings us closer to God and prepares us to fulfill His purposes. Let your heart be a sanctuary of God's grace, spotless and radiant with His presence.

Reflection Questions for the Day:

- How can I cultivate a heart that is pure and free from spiritual defilement?
- What practical steps can I take to guard my thoughts and actions against impurity?
- In what ways does living in purity help me to see and experience God more clearly?

Day 137 – τέλειος (téleios) – Perfect/Complete

Greek Word: τέλειος
English Word: Perfect/Complete
Meaning: Fully mature and complete in Christ, lacking nothing in character or faith.
Bible Reference: James 1:4 – "And let steadfastness have its full effect, that you may be perfect and complete, lacking in nothing."

Devotional Message:

The call to be τέλειος is not about achieving sinless perfection on our own but about growing into the fullness of God's image. It is a journey of becoming complete in every aspect—spiritually, morally, and relationally. As we pursue maturity in Christ, we learn to depend on His grace to fill every gap in our lives. This process involves embracing our weaknesses, allowing God to transform them into strengths, and continually refining our character through His Word and prayer. The pursuit of perfection is a daily commitment to follow Christ wholeheartedly, trusting that He will perfect what He has begun in us. As we mature, we reflect a more complete picture of God's love and righteousness, becoming better equipped to serve and lead others. Embrace the journey toward being complete, knowing that God is faithful to bring you to maturity in His perfect timing.

Reflection Questions for the Day:

- In what areas of my life do I still feel incomplete or immature?
- How can I rely more fully on God's grace to transform my weaknesses into strengths?
- What specific actions can I take today to move toward greater maturity in Christ?

Day 138 – νέα κτίσις (néa ktísis) – New Creation

Greek Word: νέα κτίσις
English Word: New Creation
Meaning: A transformed identity in Christ, where the old self has passed away and a renewed life has begun.
Bible Reference: 2 Corinthians 5:17 – "Therefore, if anyone is in Christ, he is a new creation. The old has passed away; behold, the new has come."

Devotional Message:

Being a new creation (νέα κτίσις) is a powerful testimony to the transformative work of Christ in our lives. When we accept Him, our former ways—marked by sin and separation—are replaced with a vibrant, renewed identity. This transformation is not superficial; it is a complete renewal of our mind, heart, and spirit. Embracing our new identity means leaving behind the old habits and patterns that once defined us, and stepping into the life God has designed for us. This new creation is characterized by hope, love, and a renewed purpose that radiates out into every aspect of our lives. It empowers us to live boldly and authentically for Christ, confident that we are being continuously molded by His grace. Let the truth of your new creation inspire you to live each day in the freedom and joy that only Christ can provide.

Reflection Questions for the Day:

- What old habits or mindsets do I need to leave behind as I embrace my new creation in Christ?
- How does understanding my new identity in Christ transform my approach to daily challenges?
- In what ways can I celebrate and nurture the new life that God is creating in me?

Day 139 – μυέω (myéō) – To Learn/Be Initiated

Greek Word: μυέω
English Word: To Learn/Be Initiated
Meaning: To gain deeper spiritual insight or secret knowledge, often referring to the process of being initiated into the mysteries of God's truth.
Bible Reference: 1 Corinthians 2:10 – "these things God has revealed to us through his Spirit. For the Spirit searches everything, even the depths of God."

Devotional Message:

The term μυέω calls us to a deeper level of spiritual understanding—a journey of learning and initiation into the mysteries of God's kingdom. It involves not only intellectual knowledge but a heartfelt revelation that transforms our inner being. As we study Scripture and seek the guidance of the Holy Spirit, we begin to grasp truths that were once hidden. This process requires humility, as we acknowledge that we do not know all things and must continually rely on God's wisdom. Embracing μυέω means opening ourselves to divine instruction, allowing the Spirit to impart insights that shape our character and guide our decisions. This deeper learning enriches our faith, making us more effective witnesses of God's love and power. Let your pursuit of spiritual knowledge lead you to a more intimate relationship with the One who reveals His mysteries.

Reflection Questions for the Day:

- In what ways can I seek a deeper understanding of God's truth in my daily life?
- How does the process of spiritual initiation change my perspective on Scripture?
- What steps can I take to remain open and receptive to the guidance of the Holy Spirit?

Day 140 – ἐπιτελέω (epiteléō) – To Complete/Perfect

Greek Word: ἐπιτελέω

English Word: To Complete/Perfect

Meaning: To bring to fulfillment or maturity; to finish the work that God has begun in us.

Bible Reference: Philippians 1:6 – "And I am sure of this, that he who began a good work in you will bring it to completion (ἐπιτελέω) at the day of Jesus Christ."

Devotional Message:

Το ἐπιτελέω is to trust in God's promise that the work He has started in our lives will be brought to full completion. This assurance fuels our hope, knowing that no matter our current struggles or imperfections, God is actively perfecting our character. As we journey through sanctification, we witness gradual transformation—a process where every setback is met with divine restoration. This work of completion is ongoing, requiring our continued faith and perseverance as we cooperate with the Holy Spirit. It challenges us to remain steadfast, even when the outcome seems distant, trusting that God's plan is both perfect and patient.

Embracing ἐπιτελέω encourages us to live with expectancy, confident that our maturity in Christ will one day be fully revealed. Let this promise inspire you to press on in your walk, knowing that every step is part of God's masterful work of making you complete.

Reflection Questions for the Day:

- How do I experience God's work of completion in my life today?
- What areas of my spiritual growth need further refinement and maturation?
- How can I remain confident in God's promise to perfect the work He has begun in me?

Conclusion – Sanctification

Throughout this week, we have journeyed through the process of sanctification—the work of God in setting us apart, purifying our hearts, and perfecting our lives. We began by understanding ἁγιασμός as the ongoing work of being made holy, then embraced the call to live as ἅγιος, reflecting God's own character. Our pursuit of καθαρός reminded us to maintain purity in our thoughts and actions, while the goal of being τέλειος urged us toward spiritual maturity and completeness. As new creations (νέα κτίσις), we celebrate the transformative power of Christ in renewing our identity. Through the process of μυέω, we are invited to delve deeper into the mysteries of God's truth, and finally, ἐπιτελέω reassures us that the work of sanctification will be brought to fulfillment in God's perfect timing. Collectively, these truths form a roadmap for Christian living, guiding us to a life that is increasingly reflective of our Savior's image. May you be inspired to continually submit to God's refining work, embracing the journey toward holiness with hope, perseverance, and gratitude.

Reflection Questions for the Week:

- How has my understanding of sanctification influenced my daily walk with God?
- In what specific areas of my life do I need to grow in holiness and purity?
- How can I cultivate a deeper hunger for spiritual learning and maturity?
- What practical steps can I take to live as a new creation, free from the chains of my past?
- How does trusting in God's promise to complete His work in me affect my outlook on the future?
- In what ways can I support and encourage others on their journey toward sanctification?
- What commitments will I make this week to live a life that honors God and reflects His transforming grace?

Week 21: Obedience and Discipleship.

Obedience and Discipleship: Following Christ Fully

Obedience and discipleship go hand in hand in the life of a believer. Jesus calls us not only to believe in Him but to follow Him wholeheartedly. **Luke 9:23** says, *"If anyone would come after me, let him deny himself and take up his cross daily and follow me."* True discipleship requires surrender—letting go of our own desires to walk in God's will.

Obedience is not about legalism but about love. **John 14:15** states, *"If you love me, you will keep my commandments."* When we obey Christ, we demonstrate our faith and trust in Him. A disciple listens to His voice, follows His teachings, and seeks to live as He did—with humility, love, and sacrifice.

Discipleship is a lifelong journey of learning, growing, and becoming more like Jesus. It requires commitment, perseverance, and a willingness to serve others. Though obedience may be difficult at times, it leads to deeper intimacy with God, blessings, and the joy of living in His purpose. Let us embrace the call of discipleship, walking in obedience to God's Word, so that our lives may be a testimony of His transforming power to the world.

Day 141 – Ὑπακούω (hypakoúō) – Obey

Greek Word: Ὑπακούω

English Word: Obey

Meaning: To listen to and follow the commands of God, submitting our will to His perfect guidance.

Bible Reference: Acts 5:29 – "But Peter and the apostles answered, 'We must obey God rather than men.'"

Devotional Message:

Obedience (ὑπακούω) is the heart of our discipleship, calling us to yield our lives to God's authority above all else. When we obey, we acknowledge that God's wisdom far exceeds our own and that His ways lead to life and blessing. Obedience requires a humble spirit that listens intently to God's Word and responds with immediate action. It is not always easy; sometimes it means making difficult choices or standing against popular opinion, yet it is a demonstration of our trust in Him. As we obey, we experience the peace and confidence that come from knowing we are living according to God's perfect will. Each act of obedience builds our character and deepens our relationship with our Creator. Let your life be a testament to the truth that true freedom is found in surrendering to God's loving direction.

Reflection Questions for the Day:

- In what areas of my life do I need to practice greater obedience to God?
- How does obeying God's Word change the way I handle challenges and decisions?
- What steps can I take today to listen more intently to God's voice?

Day 142 – φυλάσσω (phylássō) – Keep/Guard

Greek Word: φυλάσσω
English Word: Keep/Guard
Meaning: To watch over, protect, and preserve what is precious, especially the truth of the Gospel and one's spiritual integrity.
Bible Reference: Psalm 119:11 – "I have stored up your word in my heart, that I might not sin against you."

Devotional Message:

Το φυλάσσω means to actively guard our hearts and minds against the forces that seek to undermine our faith. It involves protecting the truths of Scripture and our commitment to Christ from the distractions and deceptions of the world. As believers, we are called to vigilantly safeguard our spiritual heritage, ensuring that nothing corrupts our witness for the Kingdom. Guarding what is sacred requires discipline, prayer, and a steadfast reliance on the Holy Spirit to alert us to potential pitfalls. It is through this constant watchfulness that we build a fortress around our hearts, making it less vulnerable to temptation. When we guard our spiritual lives, we not only protect ourselves but also preserve a light that can shine brightly for others. Let the act of keeping God's truth at the center of your life be a daily practice that strengthens your resolve.

Reflection Questions for the Day:

- What distractions or false teachings do I need to guard my heart against?
- How can I better store and protect God's Word in my life?
- What practical measures can I adopt to remain vigilant in my spiritual walk?

Day 143 – ἀκολουθέω (akolouthéō) – Follow

Greek Word: ἀκολουθέω

English Word: Follow

Meaning: To walk in the footsteps of Jesus, imitating His example and adhering to His teachings.

Bible Reference: Matthew 16:24 – "Then Jesus told his disciples, 'If anyone would come after me, let him deny himself and take up his cross and follow me.'"

Devotional Message:

Το ἀκολουθέω is to commit oneself to the lifelong journey of following Jesus in every aspect of life. This means not only learning from His words but also adopting His attitudes, values, and actions as our own. Following Christ requires a daily decision to put aside selfish ambitions and to choose a path marked by sacrifice, love, and humility. As we follow Him, we begin to see the world from His perspective, and our lives are gradually transformed by His example. This discipleship journey is both challenging and rewarding, calling us to trust in His guidance even when the path is uncertain. In every step, His presence reassures us that we are not walking alone. Embrace the call to follow Jesus wholeheartedly, knowing that His footsteps lead to eternal life.

Reflection Questions for the Day:

- In what ways am I actively following Jesus in my daily routine?
- What obstacles hinder me from fully imitating Christ, and how can I overcome them?
- How does following Jesus transform my perspective on life's challenges?

Day 144 – σταυρόω (stauróō) – To Crucify (Deny Self)

Greek Word: σταυρόω
English Word: To Crucify (Symbolically)
Meaning: To put to death the desires of the self, symbolically dying to one's old nature in order to live for Christ.
Bible Reference: Galatians 2:20 – "I have been crucified with Christ. It is no longer I who live, but Christ lives in me."

Devotional Message:

To σταυρόω means to embrace the call to die to our selfish desires and to live a life fully surrendered to Christ. This symbolic crucifixion of the self is a powerful act of obedience, acknowledging that our true life comes from God alone. As we deny the old nature and its temptations, we make room for the transformative work of the Holy Spirit in our lives. This process is challenging and often requires us to make significant sacrifices, but it is essential for spiritual growth and maturity. When we crucify our worldly ambitions, we allow Christ to take full control, leading to a life that reflects His love and righteousness. Our willingness to let go of self-centered pursuits paves the way for deeper intimacy with God. Embrace the call to cross your own self aside, knowing that in doing so, you are aligning your life with the eternal purpose of Christ.

Reflection Questions for the Day:

- What aspects of my life need to be "crucified" in order to follow Christ more fully?
- How does denying my own desires open up space for God's work in me?
- In what ways can I demonstrate a willingness to sacrifice for the sake of the Gospel?

Day 145 – δουλόω (doulóō) – Serve (Bondservant Dedication)

Greek Word: δουλόω
English Word: Serve
Meaning: To act as a servant or bondservant for Christ, dedicating one's life entirely to His service.
Bible Reference: Romans 6:22 – "But now that you have been set free from sin and have become slaves (δουλόω) to God, the fruit you get leads to sanctification and its end, eternal life."

Devotional Message:

Το δουλόω is to willingly embrace the role of a servant for Christ, dedicating every aspect of our lives to His service. This form of servanthood is not about degradation but about honoring the example of our Savior, who came not to be served but to serve others. As His bondservants, we are called to display humility, selflessness, and a relentless commitment to the welfare of others. Serving God requires us to set aside personal ambitions and to focus on advancing His Kingdom through acts of love and compassion. It is through service that we experience true freedom, as we become instruments of His grace in a hurting world. When we serve, we mirror the heart of Christ, and our lives become a living testimony to the power of sacrificial love. Embrace a lifestyle of devoted service, knowing that in serving others, you are serving the Lord.

Reflection Questions for the Day:

- In what practical ways can I serve Christ and others in my community?
- How does embracing a servant's heart transform my relationships and daily interactions?
- What steps can I take today to set aside my own ambitions in favor of God's calling?

Day 146 – ζηλόω (zēlóō) – Be Zealous

Greek Word: ζηλόω
English Word: To Be Zealous
Meaning: To display fervent enthusiasm and earnest dedication in serving God, pursuing His purposes with passion.
Bible Reference: Titus 2:14 – "Who gave himself for us to redeem us from all lawlessness and to purify for himself a people for his own possession who are zealous (ζηλόω) for good works."

Devotional Message:

To ζηλόω is to cultivate a passionate, energetic commitment to living out God's will. Zealousness for God's purposes means that our hearts burn with enthusiasm for the work of the Kingdom. It is not a superficial excitement but a deep, enduring passion that drives us to pursue righteousness and to engage wholeheartedly in service. This fervor inspires us to overcome complacency and to actively seek opportunities to glorify God in every sphere of life. When we are zealous, we invest our time, talents, and resources in advancing the Gospel and caring for those in need. It is a quality that energizes our prayers, fuels our evangelism, and strengthens our resolve in the face of challenges. Embrace ζηλόω as a daily attitude, allowing God's passion to ignite every corner of your life.

Reflection Questions for the Day:

- In what ways can I cultivate a more passionate commitment to God's work?
- How does my enthusiasm for serving Christ influence my daily actions?
- What practical steps can I take to demonstrate zeal for good works in my community?

Day 147 – παραμένω (paraménō) – Continue/Abide

Greek Word: παραμένω
English Word: Continue/Abide
Meaning: To remain steadfast, persist in faith, and continually abide in Christ despite challenges.
Bible Reference: John 8:31 – "So Jesus said to the Jews who had believed him, 'If you abide in my word, you are truly my disciples.'"

Devotional Message:

To παραμένω is to commit to a life of perseverance and steadfastness in our walk with Christ. Abiding in Him means that we stay rooted in His truth and remain connected to His love, even when storms arise. This enduring commitment calls us to a lifestyle of continual prayer, reflection, and obedience, ensuring that our faith remains vibrant and active. When we abide in Christ, our relationship deepens, and we are empowered to face every challenge with confidence and hope. This perseverance is not a one-time event but a daily commitment to live out our identity as His disciples. Let your life be characterized by an unwavering determination to remain in the light of His Word, drawing strength and guidance from the eternal love of your Savior. Embrace the call to παραμένω, knowing that in abiding in Him, you find true life and lasting peace.

Reflection Questions for the Day:

- What does it mean for me to truly abide in Christ on a daily basis?
- How can I cultivate habits that help me remain steadfast in my faith?
- In what ways can I encourage others to persevere in their walk with God?

Conclusion – Obedience and Discipleship

Throughout this week, we have delved into the heart of what it means to live as a committed disciple of Christ. We began by embracing ὑπακούω, learning that true obedience requires a willing heart and a submission to God's authority. We then discovered the importance of guarding God's truth (φυλάσσω) and following the example of our Savior (ἀκολουθέω) with dedication and courage. The call to σταυρόω challenged us to put aside our selfish desires, while δουλόω reminded us that our lives are best lived in humble service to God and others. Embracing ζηλόω sparked within us a passionate zeal for good works that further the Kingdom of God. Finally, by choosing to παραμένω, we commit to an enduring, steadfast faith that persists regardless of challenges. Together, these principles form the foundation of true obedience and discipleship—an ever-evolving journey marked by sacrifice, service, and unwavering commitment to Christ. May the lessons of this week inspire you to live boldly, serve faithfully, and continually follow in the footsteps of our Lord.

Reflection Questions for the Week:

- How has this week deepened my understanding of obedience and discipleship?
- What specific areas of my life require a renewed commitment to following Christ's example?
- How can I better guard God's truth and serve as a witness to His love?
- In what ways have I experienced the call to deny self and take up my cross?
- How does cultivating zeal for good works shape my daily interactions with others?
- What practical steps can I take to remain steadfast in my faith amidst challenges?
- How can I encourage fellow believers to embrace a lifestyle of obedience and active discipleship?

Week 22: God's Attributes.

God's Attributes: Knowing the Nature of Our Creator

God's attributes reveal His character, helping us understand who He is and how He works in our lives. He is **holy**, completely pure and set apart (Isaiah 6:3). He is **sovereign**, ruling over all creation with authority and wisdom (Psalm 103:19). He is **omniscient**, knowing all things, past, present, and future (Hebrews 4:13). His **love** is unfailing, demonstrated by Christ's sacrifice for us (1 John 4:9-10).

God is also **just**, ensuring righteousness prevails and sin is accounted for (Deuteronomy 32:4). Yet, in His **mercy**, He offers forgiveness to all who repent (Ephesians 2:4-5). He is **faithful**, keeping His promises and never abandoning His people (Lamentations 3:22-23). His **omnipresence** assures us that He is with us always, no matter where we are (Psalm 139:7-10).

Understanding God's attributes strengthens our faith and trust in Him. When we face trials, we can rest in His **peace** (Philippians 4:7). When we feel weak, we can rely on His **strength** (Isaiah 40:29). The more we know God's nature, the deeper our relationship with Him grows. Let us worship Him for who He is and live in awe of His perfect and unchanging character.

Day 148 – παντοκράτωρ (pantokrátōr) – Almighty

Greek Word: παντοκράτωρ
English Word: Almighty
Meaning: All-powerful; having unlimited authority and power over all creation.
Bible Reference: Revelation 1:8 – "I am the Alpha and the Omega," says the Lord God, "who is and who was and who is to come, the Almighty."

Devotional Message:

The attribute of being παντοκράτωρ reminds us that God is all-powerful and sovereign over every aspect of existence. His might is evident in the creation of the universe and the sustaining of life through His divine purpose. When we acknowledge God as Almighty, we are filled with awe and trust that no circumstance is beyond His control. This recognition offers comfort in times of weakness and uncertainty, knowing that the One who holds all power is working for our good. It challenges us to surrender our fears and doubts, allowing His strength to carry us through every trial. In our prayer and worship, we lift our voices to honor His omnipotence and invite His mighty presence into our lives. Embracing the truth that our God is Almighty empowers us to live boldly, confident that nothing is impossible for Him.

Reflection Questions for the Day:

- How does recognizing God as Almighty change the way I face challenges?
- In what areas of my life do I need to rely more fully on His unlimited power?
- How can I express my awe and trust in God's might through my daily prayers and actions?

Day 149 – ἀπαράβατος (aparábatos) – Immutable

Greek Word: ἀπαράβατος

English Word: Immutable

Meaning: Unchanging and constant, without deviation or error; reflecting God's perfect consistency.

Bible Reference: Hebrews 7:17 – "You are a priest forever, after the order of Melchizedek." *(This verse reminds us of the unchanging priesthood and nature of Christ, reflecting God's immutable* *character.)*

Devotional Message:

The quality of being ἀπαράβατος speaks to God's unchanging nature—a foundation of truth in a world that is in constant flux. When we encounter the immutable character of God, we are reassured that His promises and His Word remain steadfast throughout all generations. This consistency offers us a secure anchor for our faith, allowing us to trust in His guidance even when circumstances shift around us. God's unchangeability challenges us to live with integrity and reliability, mirroring His steadfastness in our own lives. As we study Scripture, we see that His character never wavers; His love, justice, and mercy are as constant as the rising sun. Embracing ἀπαράβατος invites us to place our hope in a God who is always the same yesterday, today, and forever. Let this truth fortify your heart and inspire you to live with the same unwavering commitment to His ways.

Reflection Questions for the Day:

- How does the unchanging nature of God provide stability in my life?
- In what ways can I emulate God's consistency and reliability in my actions?
- How can I deepen my trust in God's promises knowing that He is immutable?

Day 150 – ἀιώνιος (aiốnios) – Eternal

Greek Word: ἀιώνιος
English Word: Eternal
Meaning: Timeless and everlasting, without beginning or end;

indicative of God's infinite nature and eternal presence.

Bible Reference: Romans 16:26 – "but now has been disclosed, and through the prophetic writings has been made known to all nations, according to the command of the eternal God..."

Devotional Message:

The attribute ἀιώνιος invites us to contemplate the endless nature of God's existence and His eternal plan for humanity. It reminds us that our God is not limited by time or space, but is the source of eternal life and everlasting hope. In embracing the eternal nature of God, we gain perspective on our temporary struggles and are encouraged by the promise of life that extends beyond the confines of this world. His eternal presence offers comfort, knowing that His love and care are not fleeting but continue forever. This truth calls us to live with an eternal perspective, investing in what has everlasting value and purpose. It challenges us to see beyond our immediate circumstances and to trust in the promise of eternal life through Christ. Let the reality of God's eternal nature fill you with hope and inspire you to live a life that honors His everlasting kingdom.

Reflection Questions for the Day:

- How does understanding God's eternal nature influence my perspective on life's challenges?
- In what ways can I align my priorities with the promise of eternal life?
- How can I cultivate an eternal perspective in my daily decisions and relationships?

Day 151 – πιστός (pistós) – Faithful

Greek Word: πιστός

English Word: Faithful

Meaning: Reliable, trustworthy, and steadfast in keeping promises; reflective of God's consistent love and commitment to His people.

Bible Reference: 1 Corinthians 1:9 – "God is faithful, by whom you were called into the fellowship of his Son, Jesus Christ our Lord."

Devotional Message:

The attribute πιστός speaks to the unwavering loyalty and reliability of God, a quality that serves as the bedrock of our hope. His faithfulness assures us that He will never abandon us, even in our most trying times. When we reflect on God's consistent nature, we are encouraged to remain steadfast in our own commitments to Him and to one another. This trust in God's faithfulness motivates us to live with integrity and honor, knowing that He always fulfills His promises. In our relationships, our work, and our spiritual journey, His faithful presence provides a constant source of strength and encouragement. Embracing πιστός inspires us to emulate this reliability in our daily lives, becoming beacons of trustworthiness and love. Let your heart be filled with gratitude for a God who is always faithful, and let that assurance guide your actions.

Reflection Questions for the Day:

- How have I experienced God's faithfulness in my own life?
- In what ways can I demonstrate faithfulness in my relationships and responsibilities?
- What steps can I take to build trust with others by following God's example of unwavering commitment?

Day 152 – δίκαιος (díkaios) – Just

Greek Word: δίκαιος

English Word: Just

Meaning: Morally right and equitable, embodying fairness and righteousness; a reflection of God's perfect standard of justice.

Bible Reference: 1 John 1:9 – "If we confess our sins, he is faithful and just to forgive us our sins and to cleanse us from all unrighteousness."

Devotional Message:

The quality of being δίκαιος calls us to live in accordance with God's perfect standard of justice, where fairness and righteousness prevail. This attribute reveals that our God is not only loving but also supremely just, ensuring that every action is measured against His eternal truth. In a world rife with injustice and inequity, reflecting on God's justice encourages us to advocate for what is right and to treat others with impartiality and compassion. It challenges us to examine our own lives and to pursue a path that honors God's moral order. As we strive to live justly, we are empowered by His example to stand against wrongdoing and to promote equity in our communities. Embracing δίκαιος means aligning our values with God's truth, which ultimately brings healing and restoration to broken systems. Let your life be a testament to the justice of God, shining His light into the darkest corners of our society.

Reflection Questions for the Day:

- In what ways do I see God's justice reflected in my life and in the world around me?
- How can I actively pursue fairness and righteousness in my personal and professional relationships?
- What actions can I take today to promote justice as a reflection of God's character?

Day 153 – ἀληθινός (alēthinós) – True/Genuine

Greek Word: ἀληθινός

English Word: True/Genuine

Meaning: Authentic, real, and unerring in integrity; reflecting the absolute truth of God's nature and His Word.

Bible Reference: John 17:3 – "And this is eternal life, that they know you, the only true God, and Jesus Christ whom you have sent."

Devotional Message:

The attribute ἀληθινός calls us to pursue authenticity in our relationship with God and in every aspect of our lives. It speaks of a truth that is not compromised by pretense or deceit, but stands firm as the foundation of our faith. In a world where falsehoods and half-truths abound, embracing what is genuine becomes an act of courage and commitment. God's truth is the light that guides us, and as we cling to it, we are transformed from the inside out. Living authentically means being honest about our struggles, our victories, and our need for His grace. It is through this genuine expression of faith that we can build trust and foster deeper relationships with others. Let the call to ἀληθινός inspire you to live with integrity, embracing the full truth of who God is and who you are in Him.

Reflection Questions for the Day:

- In what areas of my life am I striving to live authentically before God and others?
- How can I better align my actions and words with the absolute truth of God's Word?

- What steps can I take today to cultivate a deeper sense of authenticity and integrity?

Day 154 – οἰκτίρμων (oiktírmōn) – Compassionate

Greek Word: οἰκτίρμων
English Word: Compassionate
Meaning: Full of tender mercy and concern for others; exhibiting deep empathy and care that reflects God's loving kindness.
Bible Reference: Luke 6:36 – "Be merciful, even as your Father is merciful."

Devotional Message:

The attribute οἰκτίρμων invites us to see the world through the eyes of compassion, mirroring the tender mercy of our Heavenly Father. When we embody this quality, our hearts are moved by the suffering of others, and we are compelled to act with kindness and empathy. Compassion is not merely a feeling but a deliberate choice to reach out and help those in distress. It calls us to sacrifice our comfort for the sake of others and to extend a hand of love without expecting anything in return. As we grow in compassion, we begin to reflect the character of Christ, who demonstrated ultimate love through His sacrifice. Embracing οἰκτίρμων transforms our relationships, softens our judgments, and opens us to the healing power of God's grace. Let your life be marked by genuine care and mercy, shining as a beacon of hope and love in a world that desperately needs it.

Reflection Questions for the Day:

- In what ways can I show greater compassion to those who are hurting around me?

- How does reflecting God's mercy in my actions change my interactions with others?
- What practical steps can I take today to cultivate a more compassionate heart?

Conclusion – God's Attributes

Throughout this week, we have explored the magnificent attributes of our God—His almightiness, immutability, eternality, faithfulness, justice, truth, and compassion. Each attribute not only reveals the very nature of God but also serves as a model for how we are to live our lives. Recognizing God as Almighty empowers us to face every challenge with confidence, while His unchanging nature gives us a secure foundation in uncertain times. His eternal presence reminds us that our hope is never fleeting, and His faithfulness assures us of His constant care. The perfect justice of God calls us to pursue righteousness, and His truth inspires us to live with integrity and authenticity. Finally, the compassionate heart of our Creator challenges us to extend mercy and kindness to others. May these divine attributes encourage us to reflect the image of God in our daily lives, shaping our character and guiding our actions in every sphere.

Reflection Questions for the Week:

- How have I experienced each of God's attributes in my personal life and in the world around me?
- In what ways can I allow the attributes of Almighty, Immutable, Eternal, Faithful, Just, True, and Compassionate to shape my behavior?
- How can I better emulate these divine qualities in my relationships and decisions?
- What specific changes can I make this week to reflect God's character more fully?

- How do these attributes of God deepen my trust and love for Him?
- In what areas of my life do I need to see more of God's truth and justice?

- How can I encourage others to recognize and reflect these attributes of our glorious God?

Week 23: Christ's Work.

Christ's Work: The Foundation of Our Faith

The work of Jesus Christ is the heart of the Gospel, the divine mission that brought salvation to humanity. **John 3:16** declares, *"For God so loved the world, that He gave His only Son, that whoever believes in Him should not perish but have eternal life."* Jesus came to fulfill the will of the Father, living a sinless life, dying on the cross for our sins, and rising again in victory over death.

Through His **sacrifice**, He atoned for our sins, reconciling us to God (Romans 5:8). Through His **resurrection**, He conquered death, giving us the hope of eternal life (1 Corinthians 15:20-22). Through His **ascension**, He took His rightful place at the right hand of the Father, interceding for us (Hebrews 7:25). Christ's work is not only a past event but an ongoing reality—He is our High Priest, our Advocate, and our soon-coming King.

As believers, we are called to live in response to His finished work. We walk in faith, knowing that our salvation is secure in Him. Let us proclaim His name, share His love, and live in the power of His victory, bringing glory to the One who redeemed us.

Day 155 – σταυρός (staurós) – Cross

Greek Word: σταυρός
English Word: Cross
Meaning: The instrument of crucifixion that became the symbol of Christ's sacrificial love and the means of our redemption.
Bible Reference: Matthew 27:32 – "And they crucified him, and divided his garments among them, casting lots."

Devotional Message:

The cross (σταυρός) stands as the ultimate emblem of sacrifice—a place where divine love met human sin in an act of unparalleled grace. It reminds us that Jesus willingly endured agony and humiliation so that we might be reconciled to God. On the cross, every injustice and sorrow was borne, making a way for our forgiveness and new life. This symbol challenges us to understand that true love often requires sacrifice, and that our salvation was purchased at a high cost. As you reflect on the cross, let it stir within you a deep sense of gratitude and a commitment to live in a manner worthy of the sacrifice made on your behalf. The cross also invites us to lay down our burdens and pride, embracing a life of humility and service. May the vision of the cross inspire you to carry your own crosses with hope, knowing that through them, Christ's redemptive work continues in you.

Reflection Questions for the Day:

- How does the sacrifice of Christ on the cross transform my understanding of love and forgiveness?
- In what ways can I daily lay down my burdens in light of His sacrifice?
- What steps can I take to live a life that honors the price paid on my behalf?

Day 156 – ἐσταυρωμένος (estaurōménos) – Crucified

Greek Word: ἐσταυρωμένος
English Word: Crucified
Meaning: Having been put to death on the cross; a state that signifies the complete surrender of self to God's redemptive purpose.
Bible Reference: 1 Corinthians 1:23 – "But we preach Christ crucified, a stumbling block to Jews and folly to Gentiles…"

Devotional Message:

To be ἐσταυρωμένος is to be identified with Christ's own crucifixion—a radical calling to put aside self-interest and live for His sake. It signifies that our former way of life has been put to death and that we now live under the power of His sacrifice. This reality challenges us to abandon the desires of the flesh and to embrace a life marked by selflessness and surrender. In our daily struggle, we find strength knowing that we have been crucified with Christ, and it is no longer we who live, but Christ lives in us. Embracing this truth empowers us to face challenges with courage, for our identity is no longer defined by our past or our failures. It calls us to exhibit a transformed life that reflects His love, grace, and ultimate victory over sin. May you continually be reminded that your new life in Christ is a direct result of His crucifixion and resurrection.

Reflection Questions for the Day:

- What does it mean for me to have my old self crucified with Christ?
- How can I actively live out the reality of being transformed by His sacrifice?
- In what areas of my life do I still struggle to let go of self-centered desires?

Day 157 – ἀνάστασις (anástasis) – Resurrection

Greek Word: ἀνάστασις

English Word: Resurrection

Meaning: The act of rising from the dead; the triumphant return of Jesus Christ from death, which assures believers of eternal life.

Bible Reference: Matthew 28:6 – "He is not here, for he has risen, as he said."

Devotional Message:

The resurrection (ἀνάστασις) of Christ is the cornerstone of our faith, declaring His victory over death and the promise of new life for all who believe. This miraculous event is not only a historical fact but a present reality that transforms our lives. It assures us that death is not the end, and that through Christ, we too will experience a renewal that transcends the temporal. The power of the resurrection gives us hope in the midst of despair and courage in the face of life's uncertainties. It challenges us to live with an eternal perspective, knowing that our future is secured by the risen Savior. Embracing the resurrection means celebrating the triumph of life over death and allowing that victory to empower our daily walk. Let the promise of ἀνάστασις fill your heart with joy, hope, and a bold assurance of the eternal life that awaits.

Reflection Questions for the Day:

- How does the resurrection of Christ shape my hope for the future?
- In what ways can I let the power of His resurrection transform my daily challenges?
- How can I share the joy and assurance of the resurrection with someone who is struggling with despair?

Day 158 – μεσιτεύω (mesiteúō) – To Mediate

Greek Word: μεσιτεύω
English Word: To Mediate
Meaning: To serve as an intermediary; to intercede on behalf of others, especially in reconciling them to God.
Bible Reference: 1 Timothy 2:5 – "For there is one God, and there

is one mediator between God and men, the man Christ Jesus."

Devotional Message:

Το μεσιτεύω is to step into the role of an intermediary, reflecting the unique position of Christ who bridges the gap between a holy God and a fallen humanity. Mediation is at the heart of the Gospel, as Jesus intercedes for us, offering His life as the means to restore our broken relationship with God. This calling reminds us that reconciliation is a central part of God's plan, and that through Christ's mediation, we have received forgiveness and peace. It challenges us to also be agents of reconciliation in our communities, sharing the message of hope and bridging divides among people. The act of mediating involves humility, empathy, and a deep desire to see others experience the love of God. As you meditate on this truth, consider how Christ's example of mediation transforms your interactions with others. Embrace the role of mediator by praying for unity and being a peacemaker in every sphere of life.

Reflection Questions for the Day:

- How has Christ's mediation changed my relationship with God?
- In what ways can I serve as a peacemaker and mediator among those around me?
- How can I actively work to reconcile differences and promote unity in my community?

Day 159 – ἔκχυσις αἵματος (ékchysis haímatos) – Shedding of Blood

Greek Word: ἔκχυσις αἵματος
English Word: Shedding of Blood

Meaning: The sacrificial pouring out of blood, symbolizing the atonement for sin through Christ's suffering on the cross.

Bible Reference: Hebrews 9:22 – "And almost all things are by the law purified with blood, and without shedding of blood there is no remission."

Devotional Message:

The ἔκχυσις αἵματος of Christ is a profound demonstration of God's love, where Jesus' blood was shed to atone for our sins and cleanse us from unrighteousness. This sacrificial act underscores the cost of our redemption and the depth of divine mercy. Through His blood, the barrier of sin was broken, opening the way for us to be reconciled with God. It is a reminder that true forgiveness comes at a high price—a price that Christ willingly paid so that we might be set free. Reflecting on this shedding of blood calls us to a deep sense of gratitude and a renewed commitment to live in a manner that honors His sacrifice. It challenges us to consider the immense cost of our salvation and to share that message of hope with others. Let the reality of Christ's sacrificial love inspire you to live each day with humility and a desire to serve the One who gave His life for you.

Reflection Questions for the Day:

- How does the shedding of Christ's blood impact my understanding of forgiveness and redemption?
- In what ways can I honor the sacrifice made on my behalf in my daily life?
- How can I effectively communicate the depth of Christ's sacrifice to someone who has yet to experience His love?

Day 160 – νικάω (nikáō) – To Overcome/Conquer

Greek Word: νικάω

English Word: To Overcome/Conquer

Meaning: To defeat or triumph over obstacles, sin, and the power of death through the victory of Christ.

Bible Reference: John 16:33 – "I have said these things to you, that in me you may have peace. In the world you will have tribulation. But take heart; I have overcome the world."

Devotional Message:

The act of νικάω is at the core of the Gospel message, as it proclaims Christ's triumph over sin, death, and all the forces of evil. This victory is not only historical but is also a present reality in the lives of believers who walk in the power of His resurrection. When we overcome, we do so through the strength of Christ working within us, empowering us to face any challenge with confidence. The victory of Christ assures us that no matter what battles we encounter, we are more than conquerors through Him. It challenges us to shift our focus from our weaknesses to the mighty power of God displayed on the cross and resurrected in our Savior. Embracing this conquering power fills our hearts with hope and motivates us to stand firm, even in the midst of trials. Let the assurance of victory propel you to live boldly and to overcome every obstacle with faith and perseverance.

Reflection Questions for the Day:

- How have I experienced Christ's victory in my own life?
- In what ways can I draw on the strength of His triumph to overcome my current challenges?
- What steps can I take to confidently stand as a conqueror in the face of adversity?

Day 161 – σωτήρ (sōtḗr) – Savior

Greek Word: σωτήρ
English Word: Savior
Meaning: The one who rescues and delivers us from sin and death, offering eternal salvation through His grace.
Bible Reference: Titus 2:13 – "Waiting for our blessed hope, the appearing of the glory of our great God and Savior Jesus Christ."

Devotional Message:

To recognize Jesus as σωτήρ is to embrace the profound reality that our salvation is secure in Him. As Savior, He not only rescues us from the power of sin but also transforms our lives through His love and mercy. His role as Savior is the cornerstone of our faith, providing the assurance of eternal life and the promise of His return. This truth invites us to live with gratitude and humility, always mindful that our deliverance was achieved at a great cost. It challenges us to share this hope with a world in desperate need of redemption, becoming ambassadors of the Good News. In acknowledging Jesus as our Savior, we find comfort, strength, and a renewed purpose in our daily walk with God. Let His saving work inspire you to live boldly for Him, confident that through His grace, you are forever secure.

Reflection Questions for the Day:

- How does recognizing Jesus as my Savior impact my daily decisions and outlook on life?
- In what ways can I share the hope of salvation with those who have not yet experienced it?
- What practical steps can I take to deepen my trust in His redemptive work?

Conclusion – Christ's Work

Throughout this week, we have journeyed through the powerful and transformative work of Christ, which lies at the heart of our salvation and spiritual growth. We began with the cross (σταυρός), the ultimate symbol of sacrifice, which reminds us of the love that led Jesus to lay down His life. We then explored what it means to be crucified with Christ (ἐσταυρωμένος), a call to renounce self and embrace a new life in Him. The resurrection (ἀνάστασις) offers us hope that death has been defeated and that eternal life is our promise. Through His mediation (μεσιτεύω), Christ bridges the gap between God and humanity, ensuring our reconciliation. The shedding of His blood (ἔκχυσις αἵματος) stands as a testament to the cost of our redemption, while His victory (νικάω) assures us that no power can overcome the light of His truth. Finally, recognizing Jesus as our Savior (σωτήρ) anchors our faith, reminding us that our rescue from sin and death is complete. May these reflections inspire you to live in constant gratitude, embracing the work of Christ as the foundation for a life of purpose and hope.

Reflection Questions for the Week:

- How does the understanding of Christ's work shape my identity as a believer?
- In what ways can I incorporate the truths of the cross, resurrection, and mediation into my daily life?
- How can the assurance of Christ's victory empower me to face challenges with faith and courage?
- What steps can I take to more fully live out the redemption offered by the shedding of His blood?
- How does acknowledging Jesus as my Savior transform my approach to sin and temptation?
- In what ways can I share the hope and victory found in Christ's work with others?

- What commitments will I make this week to honor the transformative power of Christ's work in every area of my life?

Week 24: Church Leadership.

Church Leadership: Serving with Humility and Purpose

Church leadership is not about power or status—it is about serving God's people with humility, wisdom, and love. Jesus set the ultimate example of leadership when He said, *"The greatest among you shall be your servant"* (**Matthew 23:11**). True leaders in the church are called to shepherd, teach, encourage, and equip believers for spiritual growth and ministry.

1 Timothy 3:1-7 outlines the qualities of church leaders, emphasizing integrity, self-control, hospitality, and sound doctrine. Leaders are to reflect Christ's character, leading not by force but by example (1 Peter 5:2-3). Whether as pastors, elders, deacons, or teachers, their role is to nurture the body of Christ, ensuring the church remains faithful to God's Word.

Church leadership is also a calling to accountability. Leaders are entrusted with the care of souls and must rely on the Holy Spirit for guidance, wisdom, and strength. As believers, we are called to respect, support, and pray for our leaders (Hebrews 13:17).

A healthy church thrives under Christ-centered leadership. May those called to lead do so with humility, and may the church, in unity, follow their guidance as they together advance God's kingdom.

Day 162 – ποιμήν (poimḗn) – Shepherd/Pastor

Greek Word: ποιμήν
English Word: Shepherd/Pastor
Meaning: A leader who tends, nurtures, and guides the flock of God's people with care and compassion.

Bible Reference: Ephesians 4:11 – "And he gave the apostles, the prophets, the evangelists, the shepherds (ποιμένες), and teachers."

Devotional Message:

The role of a ποιμήν, or shepherd, is to guide and nurture the flock with wisdom and tenderness, much like Jesus did. A true shepherd cares for every individual, offering protection, counsel, and comfort in times of need. This leadership role calls for sacrifice, as the shepherd leaves the comfort of safe pastures to seek out the lost and injured. As believers, we are reminded that effective leadership is not about power but about serving others with a humble heart. When you lead as a shepherd, you model Christ's compassion and attentiveness, ensuring that every member of the community feels valued and cared for. Embracing this calling challenges you to be both strong and gentle—a guardian who lays down his life for the well-being of the flock. Let the example of the Good Shepherd inspire you to cultivate a heart that is as caring as it is courageous.

Reflection Questions for the Day:

- In what ways can I care for and nurture those around me like a faithful shepherd?
- How do I balance strength and compassion in my leadership or relationships?
- What practical steps can I take to ensure that each member of my community feels seen and valued?

Day 163 – προϊστάμενος (proïstámenos) – One Who Leads/Rules

Greek Word: προϊστάμενος
English Word: One Who Leads/Rules
Meaning: A leader who assumes responsibility and directs the affairs of the community with authority and wisdom.

Bible Reference: Romans 12:8 – "...to lead, to serve, to encourage..." *(This verse encourages using one's gifts to lead and serve within the community.)*

Devotional Message:

The term προϊστάμενος emphasizes the call to assume leadership with both authority and servant-heartedness. Leaders in the church are called to direct the community with wisdom, ensuring that decisions reflect God's truth and purpose. This role requires a balance between exercising authority and remaining humble, always seeking God's guidance in every decision. A true leader is not driven by personal ambition but by a desire to see the body of Christ flourish. By leading with integrity and accountability, you set a standard for others to follow and create an environment of trust and mutual respect. The call to be προϊστάμενος challenges you to step into roles of responsibility, whether in formal leadership positions or informal settings within your community. Embrace this role as an opportunity to serve God and others, knowing that effective leadership transforms lives and communities.

Reflection Questions for the Day:

- In what areas of my life am I called to lead or influence others?
- How can I balance authority with humility in my leadership style?
- What steps can I take to seek God's guidance in my decisions and responsibilities?

Day 164 – ἡγέομαι (hēgéomai) – To Lead/Guide

Greek Word: ἡγέομαι
English Word: To Lead/Guide

224

Meaning: To provide direction and oversight, ensuring that others are guided along the path of righteousness and truth.

Bible Reference: Hebrews 13:17 – "Obey your leaders and submit to them, for they are keeping watch over your souls, as those who will have to give an account."

Devotional Message:

Το ἡγέομαι means to step into a role of guidance where your decisions, actions, and words help chart the course for others. Leadership in the church is about more than management—it's about nurturing spiritual growth and fostering a community that thrives on shared purpose. As a leader, your guidance must be rooted in prayer, wisdom, and an unwavering commitment to God's Word. True leadership is marked by compassion and the willingness to walk alongside those you guide, offering support during times of uncertainty. It involves listening deeply, offering counsel, and being open to learning from others. When you lead with humility and a servant's heart, you create an atmosphere of trust that encourages others to follow Christ more fully. Embrace the call to guide others, knowing that your example can light the way for a community in need of direction and hope.

Reflection Questions for the Day:

- How am I actively guiding and mentoring those around me?
- What steps can I take to ensure that my leadership is both wise and compassionate?
- In what ways can I better listen to and support those under my guidance?

Day 165 – διδάσκαλος (didáskalos) – Teacher

Greek Word: διδάσκαλος

English Word: Teacher

Meaning: One who instructs, educates, and imparts knowledge of God's truth to others, building a foundation of sound doctrine.

Bible Reference: James 3:1 – "Not many of you should become teachers, my brothers, for you know that we who teach will be judged with greater strictness."

Devotional Message:

The role of a διδάσκαλος is essential in the nurturing and development of the Church's faith. As a teacher, you are entrusted with the responsibility of communicating the truths of Scripture in a way that is both clear and transformative. Teaching is more than the transmission of knowledge—it is an act of shaping hearts and minds to align with God's will. It requires diligence, humility, and a deep understanding of the Word, as well as a passion for seeing others grow in their faith. The calling to teach challenges you to continuously learn and remain open to the guidance of the Holy Spirit. In doing so, you become a model of lifelong learning and a source of encouragement for those seeking to understand God's mysteries. Embrace the role of teacher with a commitment to accuracy, integrity, and a genuine desire to help others mature in their walk with Christ.

Reflection Questions for the Day:

- What areas of Scripture do I feel most passionate about sharing with others?
- How can I better equip myself to teach effectively and authentically?
- In what ways can my teaching contribute to the spiritual growth of my community?

Day 166 – προφήτης (prophḗtēs) – Prophet

Greek Word: προφήτης

English Word: Prophet

Meaning: A messenger who speaks forth God's word and insight, often bringing divine guidance and sometimes correction to the community.

Bible Reference: Ephesians 4:11 – "And he gave the apostles, the prophets, the evangelists, the shepherds, and teachers..."

Devotional Message:

The role of a προφήτης is to serve as a conduit for God's voice, proclaiming truths that inspire, correct, and guide the church. Prophets are called to speak with clarity and conviction, often addressing issues that require divine insight and intervention. Their messages are not just predictions but calls to action—inviting believers to align their lives with God's will. This prophetic ministry requires humility, courage, and an unwavering commitment to truth, as well as a deep sensitivity to the prompting of the Holy Spirit. When a prophet speaks, their words echo the heart of God, challenging us to examine our lives and to seek repentance where needed. Embracing the prophetic gift means being open to God's revelation, even when it calls us out of our comfort zones. Let the spirit of the prophet inspire you to be bold in proclaiming God's truth for the benefit of the entire community.

Reflection Questions for the Day:

- How can I be more receptive to the promptings of the Holy Spirit in my daily life?
- In what ways can I use my voice to speak truth and encourage others in the faith?
- How might I balance humility and boldness when sharing insights that I believe come from God?

Day 167 – ἐπίμελομαι (epimélomai) – To Take Care Of

Greek Word: ἐπίμελομαι

English Word: To Take Care Of

Meaning: To diligently and lovingly care for and oversee the well-being of others within the community.

Bible Reference: Luke 10:34 – "And he went to him and bound up his wounds, pouring on oil and wine." *(This verse illustrates compassionate care, a core aspect of ἐπίμελομαι.)*

Devotional Message:

To ἐπίμελομαι is to embrace the call to care deeply for others, ensuring their physical, emotional, and spiritual well-being. This type of leadership involves not only managing tasks but also nurturing relationships and offering personal support. It requires empathy, attentiveness, and a genuine desire to see others thrive in their walk with God. By taking care of those in our community, we reflect the heart of Christ, who cared for the hurting and the broken. This responsibility extends beyond mere duty—it is an expression of love and commitment that builds unity and fosters growth. As you take care of others, you become a vital source of encouragement and stability, making the community stronger and more resilient. Embrace this role with a servant's heart, knowing that your diligent care is a powerful testimony of God's love.

Reflection Questions for the Day:

- In what ways can I better care for the needs of those around me?
- How does nurturing others reflect the love of Christ in my life?

- What practical actions can I take to demonstrate genuine care and support within my community?

Day 168 – οἰκονόμος (oikonomos) – Steward

Greek Word: οἰκονόμος
English Word: Steward
Meaning: A manager or caretaker responsible for overseeing and administering the resources, responsibilities, and affairs entrusted to him by God.
Bible Reference: 1 Corinthians 4:1 – "Let a man so account himself as a steward of God's mysteries."

Devotional Message:

The role of an οἰκονόμος is to wisely manage the resources, gifts, and responsibilities that God has entrusted to us. This stewardship extends to every area of our lives—our finances, time, relationships, and spiritual gifts. As stewards, we are called to act with integrity and accountability, ensuring that all we have is used for God's glory and the benefit of His kingdom. Effective stewardship involves discernment, planning, and a deep reliance on God's guidance. It reminds us that everything we possess is not our own but a trust from the Creator, meant to be used wisely and generously. By embracing this responsibility, we honor God and contribute to the flourishing of our community. Let the spirit of stewardship inspire you to manage your resources faithfully, knowing that your faithful service is an act of worship to the One who is the ultimate owner.

Reflection Questions for the Day:

- In what areas of my life can I improve my stewardship of God's resources?
- How can I better manage my time, talents, and treasures to serve His kingdom?
- What changes can I make to ensure that my administration of God's gifts honors Him?

Conclusion – Church Leadership

Throughout this week, we have explored various facets of church leadership that are essential for building a vibrant, nurturing community of believers. We began with the role of the ποιμήν, a shepherd who guides and cares for the flock with compassion and strength. We then examined the responsibilities of a προϊστάμενος and ἡγέομαι, leaders who provide direction and inspire trust through wise and humble governance. As a διδάσκαλος, the call to teach is both a privilege and a responsibility, shaping the minds and hearts of those we lead. The prophetic role of προφήτης reminds us to be sensitive to God's voice and to speak His truth boldly, while ἐπίμελομαι emphasizes the importance of diligently caring for the community. Finally, as οἰκονόμος, we are entrusted with the stewardship of God's gifts, managing them wisely for the glory of His kingdom. Collectively, these principles form a robust framework for effective church leadership—one that is characterized by humility, service, and unwavering commitment to Christ. May these insights inspire you to lead with integrity and passion, nurturing a community that reflects the heart and mind of our Savior.

Reflection Questions for the Week:

- How has my understanding of church leadership evolved through these reflections?

- In what ways can I apply these principles of leadership in my personal and community life?
- How can I better serve and support those in leadership roles around me?
- What areas of my character need to be developed to fulfill a leadership role more effectively?
- How does embodying a servant's heart change the way I view authority and responsibility?
- In what ways can I encourage unity and growth within my church community?
- What commitments will I make to nurture my leadership skills and support the mission of the Church?

Week 25: Fellowship and Unity.

Fellowship and Unity: The Bond of the Body of Christ

Fellowship and unity are essential to the life of every believer. The Church is not just a gathering of individuals but a family, united by faith in Christ. **Acts 2:42** describes the early church, saying, *"And they devoted themselves to the apostles' teaching and the fellowship, to the breaking of bread and the prayers."* True fellowship is more than social interaction—it is a deep spiritual connection rooted in Christ's love.

Unity is God's desire for His people. **Psalm 133:1** says, *"Behold, how good and pleasant it is when brothers dwell in unity!"* When believers live in harmony, they reflect the love of Christ to the world (John 13:35). Unity does not mean uniformity, but a shared commitment to God's truth, mission, and love. It requires humility, forgiveness, and a willingness to serve one another.

Satan seeks to divide, but the Holy Spirit unites. As we walk in fellowship, we encourage, strengthen, and support one another in faith. Let us be peacemakers, build one another up, and work together for God's Kingdom. A united church is a powerful witness of God's love, shining brightly in a world in desperate need of hope.

Day 169 – μετοχή (metochḗ) – Participation/Sharing

Greek Word: μετοχή
English Word: Participation/Sharing
Meaning: Involvement and active participation in the life and mission of the community, sharing in its joys, struggles, and responsibilities.
Bible Reference: Hebrews 3:14 – "For we have come to share in Christ, if indeed we hold our original confidence firm to the end."

Devotional Message:

Participation (μετοχή) calls us to be fully engaged in the life of the Church, where every member contributes to the collective mission. It is about more than mere attendance—it is active involvement, sharing our time, talents, and resources with one another. When we participate, we acknowledge that we are part of a larger body, where every gift matters and every voice adds to the symphony of God's work. This shared journey enriches our faith as we experience the ups and downs together, celebrating victories and supporting each other through challenges. Participation fosters deep connections that transform the church from a gathering into a family. As you embrace μετοχή, let your commitment to community shine forth, knowing that your contributions help build a legacy of unity and hope. In doing so, you mirror the selfless love of Christ, who calls us to walk together as one.

Reflection Questions for the Day:

- How am I actively participating in my church community?
- What gifts or talents can I share to strengthen the fellowship of believers around me?
- How does sharing in the burdens and joys of others enrich my own faith?

Day 170 – ἕνωσις (hénōsis) – Unity

Greek Word: ἕνωσις

English Word: Unity

Meaning: The state of being united or joined together in purpose, spirit, and love, reflecting the oneness of the Body of Christ.

Bible Reference: John 17:21 – "That they may all be one, just as you, Father, are in me, and I in you…"

Devotional Message:

Unity (ἕνωσις) is the beautiful reflection of Christ's prayer for His followers—that we may be one in spirit and purpose. It is the thread that binds diverse individuals into a cohesive community, overcoming differences to create a unified front of love and service. True unity is marked by mutual respect, shared vision, and the willingness to work together for the sake of the Gospel. It calls us to put aside personal agendas and to embrace a collective identity rooted in Christ. In unity, our strengths are multiplied, and our weaknesses are shared, allowing us to support one another through every trial. This oneness is not forced but flows naturally when we focus on the love of God, which unites our hearts.

Embrace ἕνωσις as a core value, and let it be the hallmark of your relationships in the church.

Reflection Questions for the Day:

- How do I contribute to a sense of unity within my church community?
- In what ways can I bridge differences and promote oneness among fellow believers?
- How does the reality of our unity in Christ impact my daily interactions with others?

Day 171 – σύμμορφος (sýmmorphos) – Conformed Together

Greek Word: σύμμορφος
English Word: Conformed Together
Meaning: Sharing the same form or character; being united in thought, attitude, and purpose as a community of believers.
Bible Reference: Romans 8:29 – "For those whom he foreknew he also predestined to be conformed to the image of his Son..."

Devotional Message:

To be σύμμορφος is to be shaped into a common likeness—where the diversity of our individual experiences is united by the character of Christ. It is a call to align our hearts and minds with His example so that our community reflects His image. When we are conformed together, our collective witness becomes stronger, as we display consistency and harmony in our beliefs and actions. This process involves constant transformation as we allow the Holy Spirit to mold us into a unified body. It challenges us to set aside personal differences and to focus on the common purpose of glorifying God. Embracing σύμμορφος means valuing unity in diversity, where each member contributes uniquely while still reflecting the same Christ-like character. Let your life be a testimony to the power of being molded in the image of Christ through shared commitment and mutual love.

Reflection Questions for the Day:

- How can I contribute to a unified character within my community?
- In what areas might I need to adjust my attitudes to better align with the example of Christ?
- What practical steps can we take as a community to be more consistently conformed together in our faith?

Day 172 – συμφωνέω (symphōnéō) – To Agree/Harmonize

Greek Word: συμφωνέω
English Word: To Agree/Harmonize
Meaning: To be of one accord or to come into agreement, creating a harmonious and unified environment among believers.
Bible Reference: Matthew 18:19 – "Again I say to you, if two of you

agree on earth about anything they ask, it will be done for them by my Father in heaven."

Devotional Message:

Το συμφωνέω is to intentionally foster agreement and harmony among fellow believers, recognizing that unity in purpose amplifies the power of our prayers and witness. It calls us to listen to one another, to seek common ground, and to work together for the advancement of God's Kingdom. When we harmonize our hearts and minds, we create an environment where the love of Christ is evident in every decision and action. This agreement does not mean uniformity in all opinions, but rather a shared commitment to the core truths of the Gospel. It is through such harmonious relationships that the church becomes a strong, unified body capable of overcoming challenges and making a lasting impact. Embracing συμφωνέω encourages us to prioritize collaboration over conflict and to celebrate the diversity that enriches our collective faith. Let your efforts to harmonize with others be a reflection of the unity that Christ prayed for.

Reflection Questions for the Day:

- How do I actively seek to promote harmony in my relationships within the church?
- In what situations can I work towards agreement rather than division?
- What steps can I take to better understand and value the perspectives of others in our community?

Day 173 – ὁμοφρονέω (homophronéō) – Be Like-Minded

Greek Word: ὁμοφρονέω

English Word: Be Like-Minded

Meaning: To share the same opinions, attitudes, and purpose, fostering a unified spirit among believers.

Bible Reference: Romans 15:5 – "May the God of endurance and encouragement grant you to live in such harmony with one another..."

Devotional Message:

To ὁμοφρονέω is to cultivate a shared mindset that is rooted in the love and truth of Christ. Being like-minded does not mean that we are all identical, but that our hearts are aligned with God's purpose and that we are committed to supporting one another. When believers are united in thought and purpose, the church becomes a powerful force for good in the world. This unity of mind fosters deep relationships and creates an environment where differences are harmonized by a common goal: to glorify God. It challenges us to set aside personal agendas and to embrace a collective vision that is centered on Christ's teachings. As you strive to be like-minded with others, let the unity of the Spirit guide you in your decisions and actions. Embrace this call to mutual understanding and cooperation, knowing that together we reflect the heart of our Savior.

Reflection Questions for the Day:

- How can I better align my thoughts and attitudes with those of my fellow believers?
- In what ways can I contribute to a shared vision for our community?
- What practical steps can I take to promote a spirit of like-mindedness in my church?

Day 174 – συνδέσμος τῆς εἰρήνης (syndésmos tēs

eirḗnēs) – Bond of Peace

Greek Word: συνδέσμος τῆς εἰρήνης
English Word: Bond of Peace
Meaning: A unifying force that binds believers together in love and harmony, fostering a community marked by peace and mutual support.
Bible Reference: Ephesians 4:3 – "Make every effort to keep the unity of the Spirit through the bond of peace."

Devotional Message:

The bond of peace (συνδέσμος τῆς εἰρήνης) is the glue that holds the church together, creating an environment of unity, love, and mutual care. It represents the deep connection among believers that transcends differences and unites us under the banner of Christ's love. This bond is not easily broken; it is forged in the fires of shared experience, prayer, and a common commitment to live according to God's truth. When we actively cultivate the bond of peace, we create a sanctuary where conflicts are resolved with grace and where forgiveness flows freely. It calls us to prioritize reconciliation over discord and to invest in relationships that honor God's desire for unity. Embracing this bond transforms our community into a living testimony of the peace that Christ offers. Let the bond of peace inspire you to nurture connections that strengthen and unite, reflecting the harmonious nature of our Savior.

Reflection Questions for the Day:

- What actions can I take to strengthen the bond of peace in my relationships with fellow believers?

- How can I help resolve conflicts in a way that restores unity and harmony?
- In what ways does a strong bond of peace impact the overall health of my community?

Day 175 – συμπάσχω (sympáschō) – Suffer Together

Greek Word: συμπάσχω
English Word: Suffer Together
Meaning: To share in the sufferings and burdens of others, demonstrating empathy, solidarity, and mutual support.
Bible Reference: Romans 8:17 – "Now if we are children, then we are heirs—heirs of God and fellow heirs with Christ, provided we suffer with him..."

Devotional Message:

To συμπάσχω means to enter into the pain and trials of others, sharing not only in their joy but also in their sorrow. This act of solidarity reflects the compassionate heart of Christ, who suffered alongside humanity to bring hope and redemption. When we suffer together, we create bonds that are forged in empathy and mutual understanding. It is through shared suffering that the church becomes a true family—a place where burdens are lightened and hope is renewed. Embracing this call requires vulnerability, as we open ourselves to the struggles of others and allow our hearts to be intertwined in the journey of life. In doing so, we demonstrate that we are not isolated individuals but part of a larger, caring community. Let your willingness to suffer together be a powerful testimony of God's love and a catalyst for healing in your community.

Reflection Questions for the Day:

- In what ways can I share in the burdens of those around me?
- How does experiencing shared suffering deepen my connection with others in the church?
- What practical steps can I take to show empathy and support to someone going through a difficult time?

Conclusion – Fellowship and Unity

Throughout this week, we have explored the rich tapestry of fellowship and unity—the very essence of what it means to be the Body of Christ. We began with μετοχή, emphasizing active participation and the importance of sharing in every aspect of our community life. We then celebrated ἕνωσις, the deep unity that binds us together in purpose and love, and learned that being σύμμορφος means we are shaped together in the image of Christ. Our call to συμφωνέω encourages us to foster harmony through mutual agreement, while ὁμοφρονέω challenges us to be like-minded in our commitment to the Gospel. The bond of peace (συνδέσμος τῆς εἰρήνης) serves as a unifying force that solidifies our relationships and creates an environment of trust and reconciliation. Finally, by embracing συμπάσχω, we learn to share in both the joys and sufferings of our community, reflecting the compassionate heart of our Savior. Collectively, these principles reveal that fellowship and unity are not merely pleasant ideals but essential, lived realities that empower the church to be a powerful witness to the world. May these insights inspire you to invest deeply in relationships that reflect the love of Christ and to work actively toward a community where unity prevails.

Reflection Questions for the Week:

- How has my participation in fellowship deepened my understanding of unity in the church?
- In what practical ways can I contribute to creating a more harmonious and unified community?
- How can I support others in their journey of shared joy and shared suffering?
- What steps will I take to foster deeper connections with fellow believers this week?
- How does being part of a united community encourage me to live out my faith more boldly?
- In what ways do my actions reflect the bond of peace that unites us as the Body of Christ?
- How can I actively work to resolve conflicts and promote unity within my church and beyond?

Week 26: Encouragement and Comfort.

Encouragement and Comfort: Strength for the Journey

Encouragement and comfort are vital for every believer, reminding us that we are not alone in our struggles. **2 Corinthians 1:3-4** calls God the *"Father of mercies and God of all comfort, who comforts us in all our affliction, so that we may be able to comfort those who are in any affliction."* God's love and presence sustain us in difficult times, giving us the strength to persevere.

Life is filled with challenges, but God's Word reassures us that He is near to the brokenhearted (Psalm 34:18). His promises provide hope, and His Spirit gives peace beyond understanding (Philippians 4:7). Through prayer, worship, and Scripture, we are renewed daily, finding rest in His faithfulness.

As recipients of God's encouragement, we are also called to uplift others. **1 Thessalonians 5:11** says, *"Encourage one another and build one another up."* A kind word, a helping hand, or a prayer can make a profound difference in someone's life. Let us be vessels of God's comfort, strengthening those around us and pointing them to the hope found in Christ. In both joy and sorrow, His presence is our refuge and our strength.

Day 176 – παράκλησις (paráklēsis) – Encouragement/Comfort

Greek Word: παράκλησις
English Word: Encouragement/Comfort
Meaning: The act of calling someone to one's side to offer support, consolation, and strength during difficult times.
Bible Reference: 2 Corinthians 1:3-4 – "Blessed be the God and Father of our Lord Jesus Christ, the Father of mercies and God of all

comfort, who comforts us in all our affliction, so that we may be able to comfort those who are in any affliction, with the comfort with which we ourselves are comforted by God."

Devotional Message:

The word παράκλησις reminds us that God is our constant source of encouragement and comfort. In our moments of despair, He draws near to offer solace, much like a close friend who supports us through life's storms. This divine comfort is not fleeting; it is a steady reassurance that God's love surrounds us even in our darkest hours. When we receive this comfort, our hearts are filled with hope, enabling us to extend similar care to others. Embracing παράκλησις calls us to both receive and pass on the tender mercy we have experienced. It is a beautiful cycle of support that strengthens the bonds of our community and reflects Christ's own heart. Allow the comfort of God to embolden you today, and let that same spirit of encouragement flow through you to uplift those around you.

Reflection Questions for the Day:

- How have I experienced God's comfort in my times of need?
- In what ways can I extend the same encouragement to someone who is struggling?
- What practical steps can I take to be more open to receiving and sharing divine comfort?

Day 177 – παραμυθέομαι (paramythéomai) – To Console/Comfort

Greek Word: παραμυθέομαι
English Word: To Console/Comfort
Meaning: To offer consolation, empathy, and reassurance to

someone in distress, mirroring God's gentle care.

Bible Reference: 1 Thessalonians 2:11-12 – "For you know how, like a father with his children, we exhorted each one of you and encouraged you and charged you to walk in a manner worthy of God, who calls you into his own kingdom."

Devotional Message:

Το παραμυθέομαι is to actively reach out to those burdened by sorrow, offering a word of comfort or a compassionate presence. It involves stepping into the pain of others with empathy, much like Christ, who tenderly cared for the grieving. This comforting ministry is a reflection of God's own heart—a heart that is moved by our suffering and eager to bring relief. By consoling others, we not only honor God's command to love one another but also grow in our own ability to empathize and serve. Our words of comfort can heal wounds, restore hope, and remind people that they are not alone. Embracing this call challenges us to be sensitive to the needs around us and to be quick to offer a gentle word or a listening ear. Let the act of comforting others transform your perspective, knowing that every act of compassion points to the heart of our Savior.

Reflection Questions for the Day:

- Who in my life might benefit from my words of comfort today?
- How can I cultivate a heart that is quick to console those in distress?
- What actions can I take to be a better listener and more empathetic toward others' struggles?

Day 178 – οἰκοδομέω (oikodoméō) – Build Up/Edify

Greek Word: οἰκοδομέω

English Word: Build Up/Edify

Meaning: To strengthen, encourage, and develop others spiritually through supportive actions and uplifting words.

Bible Reference: 1 Thessalonians 5:11 – "Therefore encourage one another and build one another up, just as you are doing."

Devotional Message:

Το οἰκοδομέω is to actively participate in the growth and nurturing of the body of Christ. When we build up one another, we contribute to a community where every member is strengthened and empowered to fulfill God's purpose. This edification goes beyond simple words; it involves tangible actions that support and uplift our brothers and sisters in faith. In a world filled with discouragement, your efforts to edify can serve as a beacon of hope and a reminder of God's transformative love. The process of building up others also enriches your own spiritual journey, as you see firsthand the impact of God's work in a life renewed. Embracing this practice not only benefits individuals but creates a ripple effect that enhances the entire community. Let your actions be guided by a desire to inspire, encourage, and elevate those around you.

Reflection Questions for the Day:

- In what practical ways can I build up those around me today?
- How does encouraging others strengthen my own faith?
- What specific words or actions can I offer to support a friend or fellow believer in need?

Day 179 – παρακαλέω (parakaléō) – To Encourage/Exhort

Greek Word: παρακαλέω

English Word: To Encourage/Exhort

Meaning: To call upon someone with uplifting and motivating words, urging them to remain steadfast in their faith and actions.

Bible Reference: Hebrews 3:13 – "But exhort one another every day, as long as it is called 'Today,' that none of you may be hardened by the deceitfulness of sin."

Devotional Message:

Το παρακαλέω is to actively speak life into others by urging them to hold fast to God's promises. This form of encouragement involves both affirming the worth of those around us and challenging them to persevere in their spiritual walk. In a culture often marked by discouragement, your exhortation can serve as a lifeline to someone feeling overwhelmed by challenges. It is an invitation to lean on God's strength, reminding others that they are not alone in their journey. When we encourage, we help to dispel doubt and foster an environment of hope and resilience. This practice not only strengthens the individual but also solidifies the unity of the community, as each person is lifted by the shared love of Christ. Embrace the call to encourage with boldness, knowing that your words can spark a renewed sense of purpose and determination in someone's heart.

Reflection Questions for the Day:

- Who do I need to encourage today with words of hope and reassurance?
- How can I become more proactive in exhorting others to remain faithful?
- What practical steps can I take to ensure my words reflect the love and truth of God?

Day 180 – εὐθυμέω (euthyméō) – Be Cheerful

Greek Word: εὐθυμέω

English Word: Be Cheerful

Meaning: To maintain a positive and joyful outlook, exhibiting a spirit of gladness and optimism regardless of circumstances.

Bible Reference: James 5:13 – "Is anyone among you suffering? Let him pray. Is anyone cheerful? Let him sing psalms."

Devotional Message:

To εὐθυμέω is to cultivate an inner joy that shines forth even in challenging times. This cheerfulness is not dependent on our external circumstances but flows from the assurance of God's love and salvation. When we choose to be cheerful, we invite a light into our lives that can dispel darkness and inspire those around us. Joyful living reflects the hope of the Gospel, reminding us that our present struggles are temporary in the light of eternal promises. Maintaining a cheerful heart is an act of worship, as it praises God for His goodness even amid trials. It challenges us to look beyond our immediate hardships and to trust in the sustaining power of Christ. Let your cheerfulness be a testimony to the enduring hope that comes from a life rooted in God's grace.

Reflection Questions for the Day:

- How can I cultivate a spirit of cheerfulness, even when facing difficulties?
- What are some practical ways to spread joy within my community?
- How does embracing a cheerful attitude reflect my faith in God's promises?

Day 181 – ἀναπαύω (anapaúō) – To Give Rest/Refresh

Greek Word: ἀναπαύω

English Word: To Give Rest/Refresh

Meaning: To provide relief, solace, or renewal, offering a place of spiritual or physical rest to those who are weary.

Bible Reference: Matthew 11:28 – "Come to me, all who labor and are heavy laden, and I will give you rest."

Devotional Message:

To ἀναπαύω is to create a space where weary souls can find solace and rejuvenation in the presence of God. This act of offering rest reflects Christ's invitation to all who are burdened by life's challenges. In a world filled with constant demands and stress, providing rest is both a compassionate gesture and a powerful ministry. When you extend rest and refreshment, you become a conduit of God's grace, allowing His peace to permeate the hearts of those around you. This service not only alleviates temporary exhaustion but also nurtures long-term spiritual health. Embracing the call to give rest means recognizing the need for balance in our lives and the importance of pausing to receive God's loving care. Allow His promise of rest to guide you, and then share that restorative power with others who need a break from their burdens.

Reflection Questions for the Day:

- In what ways can I offer rest and refreshment to someone who is overwhelmed?
- How does the promise of rest in Christ influence my own approach to self-care?

- What practical actions can I take to create a peaceful environment for those in need?

Day 182 – στηρίζω (stērízō) – To Strengthen/Establish

Greek Word: στηρίζω
English Word: To Strengthen/Establish
Meaning: To provide firm support, reinforcing and encouraging someone's faith and resolve in the face of challenges.
Bible Reference: 1 Thessalonians 3:2 – "For when we were with you, we kept telling you repeatedly that we would be so supported by your faith..."

Devotional Message:

To στηρίζω means to be a source of unwavering strength and support for others, helping them stand firm in their faith. This act of strengthening goes beyond mere words; it is an active commitment to bolster someone's spirit through encouragement, prayer, and practical help. In times of trial, your support can be the anchor that holds someone steady amid life's storms. By strengthening one another, we fulfill God's command to bear each other's burdens and to build up the Body of Christ. When you dedicate yourself to establishing others in their faith, you contribute to a community marked by resilience and hope. Let your actions and words be filled with the power to encourage and fortify, reminding those around you that they are not alone in their struggles. Embrace the call to be a steadfast support, confident that every act of encouragement adds to the foundation of God's eternal kingdom.

Reflection Questions for the Day:

- Who in my life needs encouragement and support right now?

- How can I actively contribute to strengthening the faith of those around me?
- What practical steps can I take today to be a firm foundation for someone in need?

Conclusion – Encouragement and Comfort

Throughout this week, we have journeyed through the multifaceted theme of encouragement and comfort—a divine provision that sustains us through every trial and lifts us in times of despair. We began with παράκλησις, which reminds us that God's comfort is always at hand, and that we, too, are called to extend this solace to others. We learned the value of personally consoling others through παραμυθέομαι, and how actively building up one another (οἰκοδομέω) strengthens the whole community. The call to παρακαλέω encouraged us to speak life into the hearts of those around us, while εὐθυμέω inspires us to maintain a joyful outlook despite our challenges. We were reminded of the importance of offering rest (ἀναπαύω) as a tangible expression of God's tender care, and finally, we explored the role of στηρίζω in fortifying one another's faith. Collectively, these practices form a rich tapestry of mutual support that reflects the heart of our Savior, who comforts us in all affliction. May the insights from this week inspire you to be both a recipient and a dispenser of encouragement, so that the love and comfort of God may shine through you to uplift a weary world.

Reflection Questions for the Week:

- How have I experienced God's encouragement and comfort in my own life?
- In what practical ways can I extend these blessings to others in my community?

- How does maintaining a joyful and restful spirit impact my daily walk with God?
- What steps can I take to be more intentional in strengthening and supporting those around me?
- How can I incorporate regular moments of encouragement into my routine?
- In what ways does sharing comfort help to build unity within the church?

Conclusion

The study of these 182 Greek words must have opened a doorway into the rich tapestry of the New Testament, revealing layers of meaning that enrich our understanding of Scripture. Each word serves as a key to unlock the deeper nuances behind the texts we have long cherished, inviting us into a more intimate conversation with God's Word. Through this exploration, we have discovered that the language of the New Testament is not merely a historical artifact, but a living medium that continues to speak truth, challenge our assumptions, and inspire spiritual growth.

This journey through Greek not only enhances our grasp of theological concepts but also deepens our personal faith. It reminds us that every nuance in language carries profound implications for how we perceive God's character, the work of Christ, and the ongoing mission of the Church. As you reflect on the words and their meanings, you are encouraged to embrace a new level of intimacy with Scripture—one where every phrase becomes a wellspring of divine insight and every study session transforms your spiritual walk.

May this exploration inspire you to continue learning, growing, and engaging with the Bible in its original language, knowing that the richness of God's message is ever-present, waiting to be discovered anew.